CLIFFHANGER

Other books by Alan G. Barbour

AS AUTHOR

Days of Thrills and Adventure
A Thousand and One Delights
The Thrill of It All
Humphrey Bogart
John Wayne

AS CONTRIBUTING AUTHOR

In Search of Frankenstein
The Old-Time Radio Book

CLIFFHANGER

A PICTORIAL HISTORY OF
THE MOTION PICTURE SERIAL

ALAN G. BARBOUR

Introduction by Linda Stirling

The Citadel Press   Secaucus, N.J.

Dedicated to
LOUIS MCMAHON AND EDWARD CONNOR
in appreciation for many
years of mutual friendship and shared pleasures.

ACKNOWLEDGMENTS

THE AUTHOR WISHES to express his sincere thanks to the individuals and organizations listed below who supplied, through the years, the stills and information which have made this book possible.

The Individuals:

Roy Barcroft, Donald Barry, William Benedict, Spencer Gordon Bennet, Earl Blair, John Cocchi, Edward Connor, Don Danard, William K. Everson, Eric Hoffman, Ernie Kirkpatrick, Robert Malcomson, Louis McMahon, Sloan Nibley, C.M. Parkhurst, James Robert Parish, Bob Price, David Sharpe, Samuel M. Sherman, Jim Shoenberger, Packy Smith, Tom Steele, Chris Steinbrunner, Peggy Stewart, Linda Stirling, Bud Thackery, William Witney.

The Organizations:

Cinemabilia (Ernest Burns), Collector's Bookstore, Columbia Pictures Corporation, Fawcett Publications, Inc., Ivy Films, Inc. (Sidney Tager), King Features Syndicate (Carol Beltran,) Larry Edmunds Bookshop (Milton Luboviski), Marvel Comics Group, The Memory Shop (Mark Ricci), Movie Star News (Paula Klaw), The Museum of Modern Art, National Periodical Publications, Inc., National Telefilm Associates, Inc., Premium Products, Inc. (Stephen Sallay), Screen Gems, Inc., United Features Syndicate, Inc., Universal Pictures Corporation.

Third paperbound printing, 1984
Copyright © 1977 by Alan G. Barbour
All rights reserved
Published by Citadel Press
A division of Lyle Stuart Inc.
120 Enterprise Ave., Secaucus, N.J. 07094
In Canada: Musson Book Company
A division of General Publishing Co. Limited
Don Mills, Ontario
Manufactured in the United States of America
ISBN 0-8065-0669-5

INTRODUCTION

ALAN G. BARBOUR was the first to present an important, excellently documented work on the history of sound serials in his earlier book, *Days of Thrills and Adventure.* It was certainly a "thrill" for me to appear both on the cover and in that book.

Now, Mr. Barbour takes up where *Thrills* left off, with hundreds of new photographs and an expanded text, making *Cliffhanger* even more exciting and informative. I know that every serial fan and film buff will thoroughly enjoy *Cliffhanger.* I certainly did.

LINDA STIRLING
Hollywood, 1977

THERE HAS BEEN a tendency lately to take the films of the past and analyze them to the point of sheer boredom. You won't find that approach in *Cliffhanger,* for the structure of the serials is simply too fragile to withstand that sort of scrutiny. Serials were written and produced quickly for purely commercial and entertainment value, with often less than rigid regard for logical plot and character development. That the serial holds such an esteemed place in the minds of those of us who enjoyed them week after week in their original releases is more a tribute to the considerable skill and talent of dedicated directors and performers, willing to work long and hard for little financial reward, than any artistic ambitions or concerns on the part of the studios who made them.

In an earlier excursion into serial nostalgia, *Days of Thrills and Adventure,* my only intent was to try and present an entertaining picture of the color and excitement the serials gave two generations of youngsters whose Saturday afternoon sessions at the movies were, seemingly, among the most important events in their young lives. I see no reason to change that approach in *Cliffhanger.*

It has now been more than thirty-six years since I sat in the Broadway Theater in Oakland, California, in 1940 and watched my first serial chapter. I've seen several thousand chapters since then, and the wonder of those days still remains as vividly in my mind as though it were only yesterday. Film enthusiasts like myself have often been accused of "living in the past." I plead not guilty. I consider myself a realist who knows I can't return to what I genuinely feel were better times, but can still continue to enjoy the memories of the pleasures in my past. Like the security blanket grasped so tenaciously by Linus in the *Peanuts* comic strip, I find solid comfort in knowing that I, too, have something I can cling to. When the pressure mounts, when life seems at it's most irritating and trying worst, I sit back, close my eyes and suddenly, for just a few moments, it is 1940 once again and I am back at the Broadway Theater.

ALAN G. BARBOUR

Kew Gardens, New York, 1977

CONTENTS

1 THE KING

THE MAN MOST serial fans remember fondly as "The King of the Serials" frankly admits that if he hadn't needed a few extra dollars to help him get through law school, we might now be talking about Clarence Linden Crabbe, the lawyer, and not Buster Crabbe, the actor. Born in Oakland, California, on February 7, 1908, Crabbe was taken by his parents a few months later to Hawaii where he spent most of his youth and developed his considerable swimming skills. His outstanding swimming record in high school earned him a place on the United States Olympic Swimming Team in 1928. In 1932, Crabbe made the team again and won a Gold Medal for the 400-meter freestyle. Prior to the 1932 Olympics, Crabbe enrolled as a pre-law student at the University of Southern California. While a student Crabbe worked from time to time as a stunt double and bit player. Needing money, he left college for what he believed would only be one year, but soon found himself cast in the Paramount production of *King of the Jungle* (1933), a Tarzan-like tale. Crabbe did an excellent job in his debut performance and later that same year he signed with Principal Pictures to do his first serial, *Tarzan, the Fearless*. It was not an auspicious beginning. *Tarzan, the Fearless* was a decidedly unthrilling jungle adventure which dealt with a treasure, a lost city, a series of kidnappings and rescues and meandered through twelve long episodes. Adding to the problem of general boredom was the fact that Crabbe was given no dialogue. Instead of giving Tarzan the literate qualities author Edgar Rice Burroughs had created, the scriptwriters now made The Lord of the Jungle a meaningless grunter who spoke no English. The role virtually destroyed Crabbe's possibilities for major stardom since producers pictured him as strictly a physical specimen for audiences to gawk at. *Tarzan, the Fearless* was first released as a feature composed of the first few episodes; later, chapters were added to complete the full adventure.

Now seemingly typecast as a chest-beater, Crabbe spent the next three years doing a long string of B-films until *Flash Gordon* (1936). Many stars had tested for the title role (including Jon Hall who was to star in six excellent Technicolor features with Maria Montez at Universal in the forties) and Crabbe, after agreeing to

bleach his hair, got the part and was on his way to serial immortality.

Part of the charm of *Flash Gordon* was the fact that much of the script was based on the actual newspaper adventures created by Alex Raymond. Crabbe was in superb form as he battled Lion Men, Shark Men, giant "Orangapoids," and various other adversaries in his quest to stop Ming the Merciless (Charles Middleton in his most famous serial role) from destroying the world. It was fanciful adventure with rocket ships which gave young serial audiences a glimpse into a new type of screen experience. Cast as Flash Gordon's lady fair was Jean Rogers as Dale Arden, who seemed to scream and faint constantly. Many of us thought Flash Gordon would have been much better off heading for the hills of Mongo with Ming's voluptuous daughter, Princess Aura (Priscilla Lawson). However, all turned out for the best as Flash, Dale and Doctor Zarkov (Frank Shannon) returned to Earth after having witnessed Ming's supposed demise in "The Tunnel of Terror."

The commercial and artistic success of *Flash Gordon* made it almost mandatory to do a sequel. In 1938 Crabbe found himself once again soaring through space, this time to Mars, to combat his old enemy, Ming. It appeared that Ming had the ability to walk through flames, and thus escaped death in the previous serial. Now he wanted revenge and was aiming a deadly device at the Earth in order to drain off the nitrogen in the atmosphere, dooming the planet. On hand again were Jean Rogers as Dale and Frank Shannon as Dr. Zarkov, but added to the cast for occasional comic relief was Donald Kerr as a newspaper reporter called Happy. Along the perilous route of fifteen episodes of *Flash Gordon's Trip to Mars* we met such combatants as The Clay People, The Tree People, Azura, Queen of Magic (played with style by Beatrice Roberts) and an assortment of Ming's minions. This time around it appeared as though Ming was really doomed—in the final chapter he was locked in a disintegrating room by a disgruntled former aide. His task apparently completed, Flash and his party once again returned to Earth to receive a ticker-tape parade (courtesy of Universal stock footage). Audiences again were enthralled by a production that left

Buster Crabbe and Carol Hughes confront new perils in *Flash Gordon Conquers the Universe* (Universal, 1940).

them asking only one really important question: "Why did Dale change her hair from blonde in *Flash Gordon* to brunette in the second adventure?" Not even Ming could learn that secret!

As a change of pace, that same year Crabbe starred as another popular comic strip character in *Red Barry*. In this adventure Barry, a private detective, was searching for two million dollars in missing bonds. The action centered primarily around a Chinatown setting and an old theater which seemed to be continually running old vaudeville acts. Crabbe really tried his best, but the writers didn't give him anything to really work with, and *Red Barry* turned out to be an easily forgettable serial.

Having scored a resounding success with the two Flash Gordon epics, Universal decided to try another futuristic Sunday comic favorite, *Buck Rogers*. With Crabbe as Buck and young Jackie Moran as Buddy Wade, *Buck Rogers* tried hard to capture the flavor of the earlier efforts. However, even newly-designed spaceships and the use of superior villains like Henry Brandon (as Captain Lasca) and Anthony Warde (as Killer Kane) could not compensate for the fact that the script was a meaningless series of chases and dull dialogue sequences. Even Constance Moore, cast as Wilma Deering, couldn't add any charm to this dreary affair.

Universal had hoped to do a sequel to *Buck Rogers* in 1940, but when that serial failed to capture the imagination of the public they brought back their big money-making hero for the third (and final) film in the series: *Flash Gordon Conquers the Universe*. No creditable reason was given this time around as to how Ming had escaped from the disintegrating room two years earlier, but he was back in fine style. This time he was dropping a death dust called the "Purple Death" into Earth's atmosphere. Frank Shannon, as Zarkov, was back with Crabbe in this story but Carol Hughes had replaced Jean Rogers as Dale Arden. The change wasn't really that important since Hughes seemed to scream and faint just as well as her predecessor. After twelve episodes, Ming was finally destroyed when an explosive-laden rocket ship crashed into a tower in which the dictator had been locked. Although most fans believe the original *Flash Gordon* was

the best of the three, I enjoy the more polished production of this third adventure.

For the next seven years Crabbe was absent from serial screens as he starred in a long series of low-budget Westerns and features. In 1947 he returned to the weekly-adventure ranks as Captain Silver in *The Sea Hound*. Based on a comic book and radio favorite, *The Sea Hound* was the name of Silver's schooner. The enterprising skipper embarked on an adventure to an island where he encountered villains after a hidden Spanish treasure. Photographed almost entirely on location, *The Sea Hound* gave Crabbe ample opportunity to bare his famous chest and do what he liked best—swim.

Three years later he was back as Jeff Drake in *Pirates of the High Seas*. In this sea story a cache of diamonds inspired a gang of modern-day pirates to mayhem, until they were finally run to ground by Crabbe. Quality-wise, *Pirates of the High Seas* was on a par with *The Sea Hound*. Good, but not *that* good.

Crabbe completed his ninth and final serial in 1952. The uninspired *King of the Congo* found Crabbe playing a character called Thunda and involved trying to thwart the activities of a band of spies. It was almost as though Crabbe had come full circle, going from the poorly-conceived *Tarzan, the Fearless* to peaks of serial glory as Flash Gordon only to finish up in a Sam Katzman-produced cheapie like *King of the Congo*.

Those of us who love the serials owe Crabbe an enormous debt of gratitude. Without his repeated appearances at nostalgia conventions, and the playing of his *Flash Gordon* serials on television, the memory of the serial as we knew it might well have disappeared. Serials as viable screen fare have long-since outlived their commercial usefulness. Television prefers to run a *Gilligan's Island* episode for the fiftieth time rather than cater to the wants of old film enthusiasts. The sole exception to this has been the running of the *Flash Gordon* trilogy. Even as I write this, New York's public broadcasting station (WNET) has just completed running all forty episodes of Flash and his encounters with Ming. And so our appreciation and thanks are extended to Buster Crabbe, the King of the Serials, for giving us the chance to enjoy the wonderful memories.

Facing page, top, Buster Crabbe faces certain death in the static room in *Flash Gordon* (Universal, 1936).

Bottom left, Flash (Buster Crabbe) and Dale (Jean Rogers) in a romantic interlude for *Flash Gordon* (Universal, 1936). You can be assured this only a publicity shot.

Bottom right, Many fans felt that Flash (Buster Crabbe) really should have been interested in Princess Aura (Priscilla Lawson) rather than the constantly screaming Dale Arden in *Flash Gordon* (Universal, 1936).

Above, The superb cast of *Flash Gordon* (Universal, 1936) included Priscilla Lawson, Jean Rogers, Buster Crabbe, John Lipson and Charles Middleton.

Above, As comic strip detective *Red Barry* (Universal, 1937) Buster Crabbe battled with stunt star Tom Steele and plunged to certain death in a chapter ending.

Left, Death appears imminent for Buster Crabbe as *Red Barry* (Universal, 1937).

Right, Flash (Buster Crabbe) tries to protect Queen Azura (Beatrice Roberts) but her own men bomb her in *Flash Gordon's Trip to Mars* (Universal, 1938).

Below, The Clay King (C. Montague Shaw) and his men keep Flash (Buster Crabbe), Dr. Zarkov (Frank Shannon), Dale (Jean Rogers) and Happy (Donald Kerr) prisoners in *Flash Gordon's Trip to Mars* (Universal, 1938).

Above, Flash Gordon (Buster Crabbe) and Dale Arden (Jean Rogers) encounter a ring of fiery death in a chapter ending from *Flash Gordon's Trip to Mars* (Universal, 1938).

Left, Buster Crabbe was back on Mars to do battle with Charles Middleton once again in *Flash Gordon's Trip to Mars* (Universal, 1938).

Buster Crabbe as *Buck Rogers* (Universal, 1939).

Left, Buster Crabbe and Wheeler Oakman have a disagreement in *Buck Rogers* (Universal, 1939).

9

Top, Philson Ahn (Philip's brother), Buster Crabbe and Jackie Moran stand over the unconscious Wheeler Oakman in *Buck Rogers* (Universal, 1939).

Left, The evil Killer Kane (Anthony Warde) becomes a slave of his own brain-draining helmet while Buddy (Jackie Moran) and Buck (Buster Crabbe) look on in the final chapter of *Buck Rogers* (Universal, 1939).

Facing page, Buster Crabbe and Carol Hughes in *Flash Gordon Conquers the Universe* (Universal, 1940).

12

Top left, Buster Crabbe and Carol Hughes battle Charles Middleton's deadly robots in *Flash Gordon Conquers the Universe* (Universal, 1940).

Bottom left, In *The Sea Hound* (Columbia, 1947) Buster Crabbe is about to be torn apart in a chapter ending.

Top right, Buster Crabbe bares his torso in a serial for the last time in *King of the Congo* (Columbia, 1952).

Bottom right, Terry Frost goes after Buster Crabbe in *Pirates of the High Seas* (Columbia, 1950).

13

THE QUEST FOR sudden and easy riches that led to the destruction of many a serial villain was equally (though decidedly less criminally) on the minds of the rash of enterprising young entrepreneurs who rushed into motion picture production and distribution at the beginning of the twentieth century. In less than a dozen years there were thousands of nickelodeons and movie palaces dotting America's landscapes. An immediate problem arose as to how to satisfy the demands of theater owners for new product—especially product which could draw fans to one person's establishment at the expense of a competitor's.

For their answer to this problem, the Edison Company turned to the pages of a popular newspaper, *McClure's Ladies World*, which was featuring a series of adventure stories called *What Happened to Mary?* The movie company and the newspaper entered into an arrangement whereby a series of one-reel films would be released simultaneously with a fictionized novel in the paper on a monthly basis for a year. So it was that in 1912 *What Happened to Mary?* became not only the screen's first serial, but the first example of what has become a traditional movie commercial ploy, the "tie-in." The results were very successful and encouraged the studio to continue making serials for many years. Unlike the "cliffhanger" serials we remember fondly, these first attempts were more like television shows. Each story was complete within a single episode and a broad general framework tied the entire series together. As a serial, *What Happened to Mary?* with popular Mary Fuller as the heroine, wasn't really much to shout about. Episodes like "Mary in Stageland," "A Clue to Her Parentage," and "The High Tide of Misfortune" were trivial affairs that found Mary, an orphan left on a stranger's doorstep, trying to create some kind of meaningful life for herself. In 1913 Edison turned out a sequel, again starring Fuller, called *Who Will Marry Mary?* That same year, however, beautiful young Kathlyn Williams and Tom Santschi (known as one of the combatants in the famous fight scene in the silent version of *The Spoilers)* teamed to make what many consider the first real action approach to serials: *The Adventures of Kathlyn.* Although these episodes were also complete little vignettes, the storyline was more fanciful as

Kathlyn faced the perils of wild animals and wicked enemies in pursuit of a title she had inherited in India.

In 1914, the serial finally established itself as an important genre with the production of *The Perils of Pauline.* Released in twenty episodes, *The Perils of Pauline* immediately captured the imagination of the public as star Pearl White engaged in thrill after thrill in her quest to prevent villain Paul Panzer from stealing her rightful inheritance. So popular were the young star's exploits on screen that even a song, "Poor Pauline," achieved success in conjunction with the film's release. By any critical standards *The Perils of Pauline* is a very poor serial. Almost amateurishly directed by Louis Gasnier and Donald MacKenzie, the meandering episodes are often ludicrous. One incredible sequence showed Pearl running down a steep hill with an unbelievably large (and obviously fake) boulder in threatening pursuit. Since the quality simply was not there, we must then assume that the fame of *The Perils of Pauline* rests considerably more with the charismatic Pearl White's image than with the film itself. White had been working in films since 1910, but her place in cinema history was firmly established when she accepted a $250-a-week contract from Pathé in 1914 and became the serial's most famous heroine. Many of White's later serials, like *The Exploits of Elaine* (1914) (in which she was menaced by The Clutching Hand), *The New Exploits of Elaine* (1915), *The Iron Claw* (1916), *Pearl of the Army* (1917) and *Plunder* (1923) were much more colorful and exciting as the young star faced more inventive serial perils under better directors.

Although Pearl White was the biggest serial star in silent films, she did not have the field entirely to herself. There were several other venturesome young actresses who also garnered affectionate followings. Helen Holmes and Helen Gibson alternated as stars in a series of more than a hundred one-reel railroad adventures grouped under the overall title, *The Hazards of Helen.* In reels with titles like *The Engineer's Honor, A Fiend at the Throttle,* and *A Girl Telegrapher's Nerve,* the two stars did every possible thing one could ever hope to do with trains. After *The Hazards of Helen,* which was released beginning in 1914, Holmes was later to do solo work in tales like *The Girl and the*

Left, The screen's most famous silent serial heroine, Pearl White, in a scene from *The Black Secret* (Pathé, 1919) in which she shared acting honors with Walter McGrail.

Game (1915), *Lass of the Lumberlands* (1916) and *The Railroad Raiders* (1917).

Pearl's closest rival was Ruth Roland. Backed by skilled directors and solid production values, Roland's serials were vastly superior in style and content and she was a much more exciting personality to watch in action. She justly earned the twenties' title "Queen of the Thriller Serials." In *The Red Circle* (1915), *The Neglected Wife* (1917), *The Adventures of Ruth* (1919), *The Tiger's Trail* (1919), *Ruth of the Rockies* (1920) and *Ruth of the Range* (1932), Roland dazzled audiences with an exciting parade of perilous derring-do.

Allene Ray made a fetching heroine in serials like *The Fortieth Door, Galloping Hoofs* and *Ten Scars Make a Man* in the mid-twenties, but gained much more fame co-starring with stuntman-actor Walter Miller in a series of superior serial stories like *The Green Archer, Play Ball, Sunken Silver, The House without a Key* and *Snowed In.*

Other feminine aspirants to lesser serial fame included Eileen Sedgwick, Louise Lorraine, Grace Cunard, Neva Gerber and Helen Ferguson, all of whom faced many a cinema danger to give audiences a few thrills for their money.

Although the women seem to have captured the spotlight when reminiscing about silent serials, there was a small group of male action stars who really provided the genuine thrills associated with the serial format. Joe Bonomo, Eddie Polo, Jack Mulhall, William Desmond, Jack Daugherty, Ben Wilson, William Duncan and Franklyn Farnum (among others) had loyal legions of fans who vicariously enjoyed every single daredevil exploit.

Some of the best-remembered serials of the period, though not necessarily the best-produced, featured many of the most prominent real-life heroes in fictional cinema adventures. Jack Dempsey, the World Heavyweight Boxing Champion, appeared in *Daredevil Jack* (1920), an entertaining tale that found Jack helping co-star Josie Sedgwick find some secret oil deposits. Gene Tunney, Dempsey's opponent in the famous "long count" title fight, turned up in *The Fighting Marine* (1926), a story which found him protecting a young Englishwoman in a mining town and engaging in a seemingly endless series of fights in order to demonstrate his pugilistic abilities. A boxer from an earlier era made an appearance in *The Midnight Man* (1919) in the person of James J. ("Gentleman Jim") Corbett in a slight tale that was generally written to exploit the athletic abilities of the star. Even the world's most famous magician, Harry Houdini, gave serials a single fling in *The Master Mystery* (1919), an escapade that found Houdini playing a Justice Department official bent on cracking a criminal combine intent on controlling rare patent rights. Adding to the inventiveness of the plot of *The Master Mystery* was a bullet-proof robot, a prototype of later serial automatons.

Among the dozens of prominent writers, directors and producers who brought credit to the serials, two men who really must receive attention are writer Frank Leon Smith and director Spencer Gordon Bennet. Smith was responsible for crafting the screenplays of many outstanding productions like *Sunken Silver, Play Ball, The Green Archer* and *Snowed In.* By a happy coincidence, Spencer Bennet had the good fortune to direct many of Smith's works. Fans were particularly appreciative of *Snowed In* (which featured a mystery villain who kept making appearances from Room 28 in an abandoned wilderness hotel) and *The House without a Key* (an adaptation of the first Charlie Chan novel), both of which Bennet directed with unusual skill and ability. Bennet has had a long and distinguished career. Beginning as a stuntman and actor, he finally decided that life behind the cameras was more exciting, and he did serials from silents to the final Columbia production, *Blazing the Overland Trail* (1956). Now in his eighties, Bennet continues to be in excellent physical condition and enjoys the well-deserved homage paid to him by fans for the volume of creative action material he directed.

Of the more than 270 silent serials produced, fewer than 20 (in whole or part) have managed to survive celluloid decomposition as the old nitrate stock turned to dust. The wonderful memories conjured up in the minds of the faithful who saw the silents in original release today exist only as that—wonderful memories.

Top, A scene from *The Perils of Pauline* (Pathé, 1914) in which Crane Wilbur comes to the aid of Pearl White.

Right, Tom Santschi and Kathlyn Williams in the first real serial, *The Adventures of Kathlyn* (Selig, 1913).

Far right, Mary Fuller in the series that began it all, *What Happened to Mary?* (Edison, 1912).

Pearl White and Wally Oettel in *Plunder* (Pathé, 1923).

Natalie Kingston and Jay Wilsey were the stars of *The Pirate of Panama* (Universal, 1929).

Frank Lackteen and Allene Ray were at odds in *The Green Archer* (Pathé, 1925).

Above right, Gladys McConnell and Hugh Allan seek help in *The Fire Detective* (Pathé, 1929).

Below, Walter Miller searches for a hidden treasure in *Sunken Silver* (Pathé, 1925).

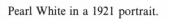
Pearl White in a 1921 portrait.

For a while Ruth Roland rivaled Pearl White's popularity in serials like *The Timber Queen, White Eagle* and *Haunted Valley.*

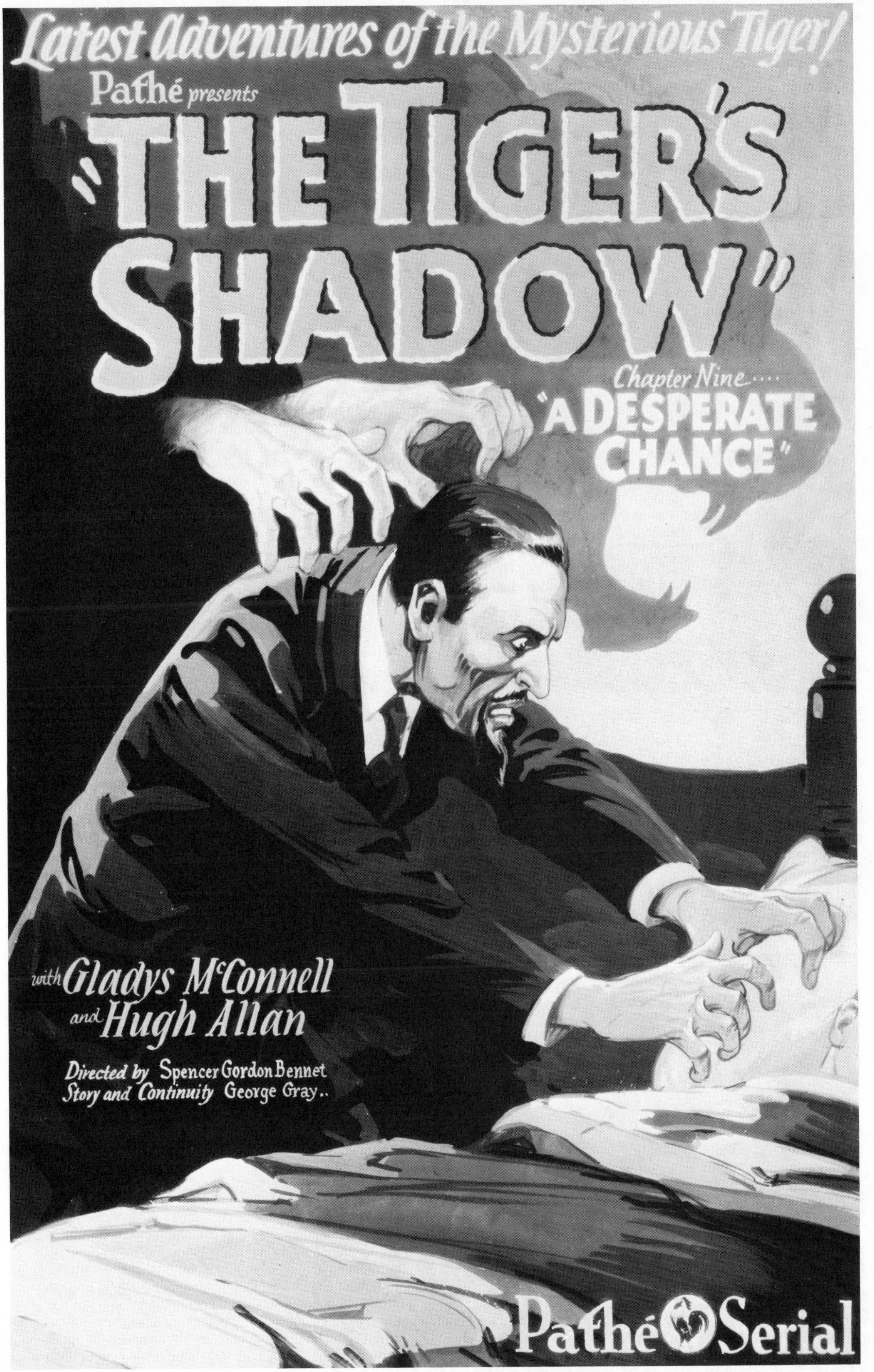
Latest Adventures of the Mysterious Tiger!
Pathé presents
"THE TIGER'S SHADOW"
Chapter Nine....
"A DESPERATE CHANCE"
with Gladys McConnell
and Hugh Allan
Directed by Spencer Gordon Bennet
Story and Continuity George Gray..
Pathé Serial

Above, Allene Ray finally gets her hands on the mysterious subject matter of *The Black Book* (Pathé, 1929).

Pathéserial

"MARK OF THE FROG"

by EDGAR WALLACE
with
Donald Reed and Margaret Morris

Directed by ARCH B. HEATH

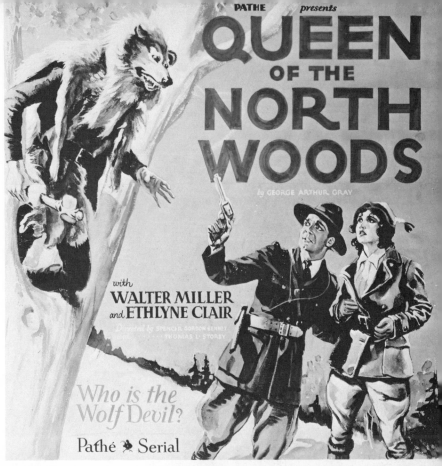

Below, Bruce Gordon and Allene Ray found many mysteries as they sought out *The Fortieth Door* (Pathé, 1924).

THE CHAOTIC TRANSITION period in the late twenties and early thirties from silent films to sound would prove to be a real test for the serial as a viable film form. Whereas dozens of companies had turned out the non-talking cliffhangers, now only Universal and Mascot were left, with an occasional independent release of usually inferior quality. There was still an audience out there for the product, but the question was: Was it worth it? The serials had peaked in the mid-twenties and were now definitely losing popularity.

Universal, which had a better physical plant and more money to work with, should have turned out a superior product. However, this was not the case. Their first official all-talking serial (also released as a silent) was *The Indians Are Coming* starring the very popular Tim McCoy. It was a meaningless mishmash, full of all-too-obvious stock footage from their silent library. Titles like *Finger Prints* with Kenneth Harlan, *Heroes of the Flames* with Tim McCoy and *Spell of the Circus* with Francis X. Bushman were similarly uninspired and represented a lack of creative enthusiasm on the studio's part. Some of these boring serials did have their funny moments, though, as in the case of *Battling with Buffalo Bill* with Tom Tyler. At the beginning of each chapter an old-timer standing in front of a shack with a horse tied up nearby would recap what had gone on in the previous chapter. Obviously filmed all at one time, as each chapter progressed the horse became more and more restless, until right in the middle of one of the old-timer's speeches the horse walked in front of the man, temporarily blocking him. In the next chapter the horse was gone, only to return a couple of chapters later. Universal was even too cheap to reshoot that one brief sequence. In fact, we can forget most of the Universal serials up until about 1934. After that bleak period the studio began to take more of an interest and began to produce quality Westerns with Buck Jones and Johnny Mack Brown, and a superior parade of serials featuring comic strip favorites Flash Gordon, Tailspin Tommy, Buck Rogers and many others.

By any standards, Mascot serials were done on a shoestring budget. However, Mascot had the one ingredient Universal seemed to lack: imagination! In less than

five years Mascot presented some well-established stars and introduced a few who were destined for bigger and better things.

Among these Mascot stars was a tall youngster by the name of John Wayne. Wayne had already made appearances in fifteen features (including *The Big Trail* in which the stardom he should have achieved somehow eluded him) before Nat Levine signed him in 1932 for Mascot's *The Shadow of the Eagle*. In the film Wayne was a skywriter in pursuit of the mysterious Eagle who had been threatening the officers of a large corporation. In these serials, Wayne had ample opportunity to demonstrate his athletic prowess. In *The Hurricane Express* (1932) he was in search of yet another masked villain, The Wrecker, who was able to disguise himself as any number of different people in a wide circle of suspects. Motorcycles, trains, planes—the writers included all forms of fast-moving danger and Wayne probably never worked harder in his life. After appearances in ten low-budget feature films, Wayne was back again as a pilot in his third and final Mascot serial, *The Three Musketeers* (1933). Tracking down masked villains had apparently become a habit since this time he was after a scheming desert marauder known only as El Shaitan.

Another future major star who took a one-time fling at the serials was dashing George Brent. He played second fiddle to Rin Tin Tin in *Lightning Warrior,* a 1931 opus which chronicled the devious machinations of a mystery man known as The Wolf Man, who was threatening a band of settlers in order to get their land.

Among the many stars also featured in Mascot serials during the early thirties were: Bela Lugosi, slinking around as a possible suspect to be *The Whispering Shadow;* veteran western star Harry Carey in an interesting adaptation of *Last of the Mohicans* and as his traditional cowboy self in *The Vanishing Legion* and *The Devil Horse;* Bob Steele, one of the great cowboy stars, incongruously cast as a pilot chasing a masked villain called The Black Ace in *Mystery Squadron;* Grant Withers in the excellent *The Fighting Marines,* hot on the trail of the mysterious Tiger Shark; Tom Tyler, another saddle ace, in the very disappointing *The Phantom of the West* and football great

Left, Bela Lugosi had a marvelous time as Frank Chandler (Chandu) in *The Return of Chandu* [*the Magician*] (Principal, 1934). Maria Alba was Lugosi's love interest, the Princess Nadji.

Harold "Red" Grange in *The Galloping Ghost*, the title referring to his famous nickname.

George J. Lewis, who was to play villains in so many future serials, remembers that when he did the lead in *The Wolf Dog* for Mascot he "never worked harder in my life." Sixteen hour workdays were commonplace, and for very small wages.

Mascot was also the last stop for one cowboy great and the first for another who would become great. In *The Miracle Rider*, the legendary Tom Mix was after Charles Middleton who coveted valuable deposits of an explosive called X-94. Unfortunately, these deposits happened to be on Indian land, so conflict ensued. Though Tom was beginning to look his age, he still carried his role off well, but it was to be his final starring screen appearance. That same year a new young cowboy singer named Gene Autry made an interesting futuristic serial called *Phantom Empire*. Gene had his hands full: each day he raced from an underground city called Murania to his ranch where he broadcast a song to fulfill a radio contract. Only a year earlier Gene and Smiley Burnette played bit parts in Ken Maynard's Mascot serial, *Mystery Mountain*, in which Maynard sought to unmask The Rattler; in the feature *In Old Santa Fe* (another vehicle starring Maynard) Gene had sung a few songs. Now he was on his way to becoming America's most famous singing cowboy.

The fifteen independently-produced serials released between 1930 and 1937 ranged in quality from the imaginative and entertaining to the downright embarrasing. Most serial buffs agree that the worst sound serial ever made was *The Lost City*. This Krellberg release had a plot in which William "Stage" Boyd ruled a hidden jungle city and created an army of giant black slaves by stretching normal-sized natives by means of a devilish device. The giants went around rolling their eyes and grunting, when they weren't screaming. Even though the very capable Kane Richmond played the lead, the direction by Harry Revier made everyone look like a poor, grade school performer. When a New York television station once attempted to run it in the fifties, protests came in so quickly that it was immediately yanked.

At the other end of the spectrum was the Bela Lugosi serial, *The Return of Chandu (the Magician)*. Lugosi had made an earlier appearance in *Chandu, the Magician* for Fox Films but Edmund Lowe had been the star of that well-done feature. Now Lugosi had his turn to combat the black magic Cult of Ubasto on the magic island of Lemuria and to free the Princess Nadji from her captors. It was all entertaining fun with excellent music and inventive sets. The serial was later edited into two feature versions which frequently played in rerun houses as a dual bill: *The Return of Chandu* and *Chandu On the Magic Isle*.

Another excellent serial was *The New Adventures of Tarzan* starring Herman Brix as the celebrated ape man. The film was actually shot in Guatemala, where Brix suffered no end of personal misfortune and discomfiture to complete a film made under extremely primitive conditions. This serial was also edited into two feature versions: *The New Adventures of Tarzan* and *Tarzan and the Green Goddess*.

There were other serials that were interesting, like *The Clutching Hand* and *The Black Coin*, and some that were awful, like *Young Eagles, Queen of the Jungle* and *Mystery Trooper*. In the vast middleground of so-so material could be found *Blake of Scotland Yard* and *Shadow of Chinatown* as well as two boring Westerns, *The Last Frontier* (in which Spencer Bennet directed a usually late, and often drunk, Lon Chaney, Jr.) and *Custer's Last Stand*.

All in all, the early thirties presented serial fans with a wide divergence of material. But the time had come for a change. In 1936 Republic Pictures (formed by the merger of Mascot, Monogram and Liberty Pictures) began to produce a new series of action serials that in a few years made the Saturday afternoon serial a commercial cinema force. Republic began with a Clyde Beatty effort called *Darkest Africa* and in the next twenty years turned out sixty-five more productions that ranged in quality from good to unforgettable.

A year later, Columbia Pictures decided to enter the field, also beginning with a jungle adventure, *Jungle Menace*, which starred the world-renowned animal trapper and trainer, Frank Buck. Columbia continued making serials for twenty years, churning out another fifty-six titles, many of which were laughable, but almost all of which were fun.

Right, A youthful John Wayne and Ruth Hall in *The Three Musketeers* (Mascot, 1933). This was the last of his three starring serials.

Below, In *Burn 'Em Up Barnes* (Mascot, 1934) Jack Mulhall was frequently at odds with Stanley Blystone (left) and Al Bridge.

Top, As Craig Kennedy, Jack Mulhall finds something he hadn't counted on in *The Clutching Hand* (Weiss-Mintz, 1936).

Bottom left, The Lightning Express (Universal, 1930) was one of those transitional serials that was released both in silent and sound versions. Petite Louise Lorraine was the leading lady.

Bottom right, Silent serial star William Desmond gave stunt ace Richard Talmadge a helping hand in *Pirate Treasure* (Universal, 1934).

Below, Robert Warwick surprises The Eagle (Robert Livingston) to the delight of Fred Kohler in *The Vigilantes Are Coming* (Republic, 1936).

Bottom, Director Mack V. Wright gives Mamo Clark and John Piccori some direction while the script boy (soon-to-be-director William Witney) checks the script of *Robinson Crusoe of Clipper Island* (Republic, 1936).

METROPOLITAN PICTURES present

"KING"
EMPEROR OF ALL DOGS in
"THE SIGN OF THE WOLF"

A SMASHING TEN EPISODE ACTION SERIAL!
with
REX LEASE · VIRGINIA BROWN FAIRE
JOE BONOMO · JACK MOWER · JOSEPHINE
HILL · AL FERGUSON · ROBERT WALKER
EDMUND COBB · HARRY TODD
Directed by
HARRY WEBB and FORREST SHELDON

EPISODE 1
DRUMS of DOOM

NAT LEVINE presents

RIN·TIN·TIN

EPISODE 2
"THE FUGITIVE"

in

"The Lone Defender"
A Stirring All-Talking Serial in 12 Chapters...

30

SYNDICATE PICTURES
present

EPISODE SEVEN
"THE DEATH TRAIL"

"The MYSTERY TROOPER"

Featuring
BUZZ BARTON
ROBERT FRAZER
BLANCHE MEHAFFEY
AL FERGUSON
CHARLES KING
"RED EAGLE"
AND
"WHITE CLOUD"
THE WONDER HORSE

·

Produced by
WONDER PICTURES

·

Directed by
STUART PATON

AN ALL-TALKING SERIALPLAY

GEORGE M. MERRICK
Presents

THE CLUTCHING HAND

a Craig Kennedy Thriller
in fifteen chapters
from the novel by
ARTHUR B. REEVE

CHAPTER 12 HIDDEN DANGER

with
JACK MULHALL · WILLIAM FARNUM
RUTH MIX · MARION SHILLING
YAKIMA CANUTT

Directed by ALBERT HERMAN
Distributed by
STAGE and SCREEN Productions, inc

Robert Kortman is about to give Harry Carey quite a surprise in *Last of the Mohicans* (Mascot, 1932).

Jack Mulhall shows Guinn "Big Boy" Williams and Bob Steele an important clue in *Mystery Squadron* (Mascot, 1933).

Herman Brix was excellent starring as The Lord of the Jungle in *The New Adventures of Tarzan* (Dearholt-Stout and Cohen, 1935). Filmed on location in Guatemala, Brix suffered illnesses and injuries but still completed the film.

In probably the worst and most offensive serial ever made, Claudia Dell prevents Sam Baker from strangling Kane Richmond in this scene from *The Lost City* (Krellberg, 1935).

Hero George J. Lewis takes on Stanley Blystone (left), Yakima Canutt (right) and Tom London in *The Wolf Dog* (Mascot, 1933).

Left, John Wayne seems to have things well in hand as he covers Al Ferguson, Charles King, Ernie Adams and Glenn Strange in *The Hurricane Express* (Mascot, 1932).

Right, As Eddie Cobb looks on, the robot immobilizes Ada Ince after having temporarily disposed of hero Onslow Stevens in *The Vanishing Shadow* (Universal, 1934).

Below left, Married to each other in real life, James Flavin and Lucile Browne solved *The Airmail Mystery* (Universal, 1932) on the screen.

Below right, George Brent was among the few actors who fought their way out of the serials and into the big features. Here, in *The Lightning Warrior* (Mascot, 1931) he shows an important clue to Georgia Hale while Rin Tin Tin looks on.

Bottom, Rin Tin Tin, Jr. comes to the aid of Kane Richmond in *The Adventures of Rex and Rinty* (Mascot, 1935).

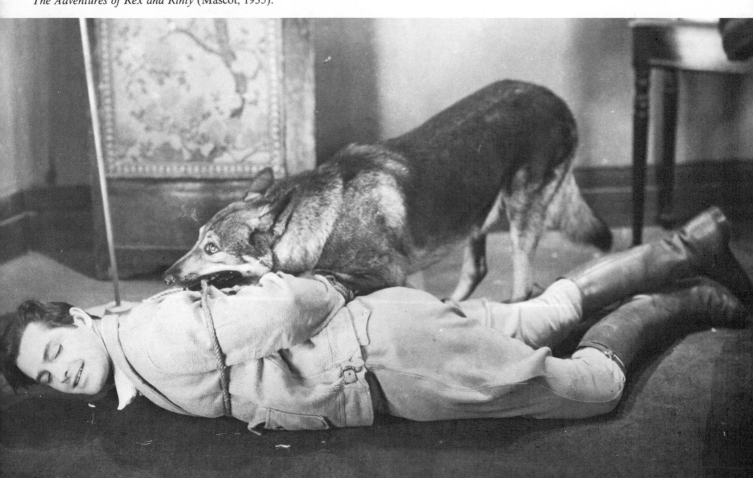

Right, One of the secrets of Republic's success was the studio's use of excellent miniatures like this dirigible and plane used in *Robinson Crusoe of Clipper Island* (Republic, 1936).

Below, Herman Brix and Joan Barclay tie up an unconscious Charles King in *Shadow of Chinatown* (Victory, 1936).

One of those rare cases where the actor and the role are
completely unified: Ralph Byrd as *Dick Tracy* (Republic, 1937).

4 "GET ME TRACY"

No ONE CAN dispute the fact that Sherlock Holmes is the world's most famous literary detective, but for more than forty-five years Chester Gould's comic strip creation, *Dick Tracy,* has been giving the celebrated sleuth a good run for the title. Indeed, Gould intended to make Tracy the American counterpart of the British sleuth.

The newspaper adventures of Dick Tracy began on Sunday, October 4, 1931, in the pages of the *Detroit Mirror.* Six years later Tracy was debuting in the first of four serials produced by Republic Pictures. In this first adventure Tracy matched wits with a grotesquely-masked villain who called himself The Lame One, and also, on occasion, The Spider. A criminal gang was unleashing a barrage of terrorist attacks on vital industries and Tracy was assigned the task of bringing the reign of terror to an end. *Dick Tracy* had one of the most frightening scenes to ever appear in a serial when, in Chapter One, The Lame One stalks a terrified Byron Foulger down a dark and deserted street and murders him. Other unusual plot twists found an operation being performed on Tracy's brother, converting him into one of the Lame One's henchmen, and the use of a futuristic Flying Wing to transport the Spider gang on their missions. The Flying Wing was a special effects creation of Howard and Theodore Lydecker, Republic's resident wizards in the creation of miniatures. The Flying Wing was so impressive that the studio used it again in *Fighting Devil Dogs* as the main source of transportation for the mysterious Lightning. Although *Dick Tracy* was entertaining, the production still showed a lack of polish. The actors wore a bit too much make-up, and there were long stretches with little action. The one really big plus was the selection of Ralph Byrd to play Tracy. Unfortunately for him, he was so identified with the role that he found it increasingly difficult to find work in later years. However, for the serial buff Byrd as Tracy was a match made in cinema Heaven.

Byrd returned as Tracy a year later in a brand new adventure called *Dick Tracy Returns.* This time around Tracy was after the notorious Pa Stark (played by Charles "Ming the Merciless" Middleton) and his evil brood of five larcenous sons. The opening episode of *Dick Tracy Returns* was as shocking as the opening of *Dick Tracy.*

Young David Sharpe, playing a new police recruit graduate, is brutally gunned down by one of Pa's sons. Sharpe, not quite dead but paralyzed, is placed in an iron lung. Pa Stark sneaks into the hospital and sadistically unplugs the iron lung, dooming young Sharpe. That was pretty vicious stuff to feed an audience composed primarily of young kids.

As the story progresses, Pa Stark's boys are eliminated one by one until only Pa remains in the last chapter. Trapped, he uses Tracy as a shield and forces him to take off in a plane. Once airborne, Tracy manages to bail out and the plane and Stark plunge to a flaming finale.

Part of the fun of these late thirties Republic serials was the frequent use of exterior location shooting. It was always a delight to see chases through deserted gas plants, lumber yards and the like. As World War II approached less and less outdoor shooting was done, both to conserve time and unnecessary travel expense. The serials suffered because of these later restrictions, and the rear process screen all too soon became a way of life at Republic.

With Pa Stark and his boys gone, Tracy took another year off and reappeared, again with Byrd, in *Dick Tracy's G-Men.* Not to be outdone by previous plots, *Dick Tracy's G-Men* began by bringing a dead man back to life. In the opening episode Tracy captures the international spy Zarnoff (played by the gifted actor and director Irving Pichel) and sees him executed in the gas chamber. His body is then quickly hijacked by members of his gang and they revive him by means of some powerful drugs. Almost immediately Zarnoff is back at work trying to sabotage America's defense system.

In this action-packed serial, Tracy battles his way out of trap after trap. One particularly exciting climax found Tracy fighting beneath a huge suspended pile of lumber which began to descend, apparently putting an end to Tracy once and for all. Another ending found Tracy transferring from a plane to a motorboat loaded with high explosives, that carried him to what seemed to be certain destruction. In the final episode Tracy is flying Zarnoff across a desert when suddenly their plane is forced down. Tracy and his prisoner start walking across the barren expanse. Literally dying of thirst, the pair come upon a spring. Zarnoff, catching the detective unaware, knocks him out, ties him up and drinks deeply and satisfyingly at the refreshing pool of water. Later Tracy is rescued and we discover that Zarnoff has poisoned himself by drinking at an arsenic spring.

Byrd's fourth and final appearance in a Tracy serial was the 1941 production of *Dick Tracy vs. Crime, Inc.* Although there was only a nominal amount of creative exterior location shooting, many fans find this particular Tracy adventure the most ingenious of the lot. A master criminal known as The Ghost has the ability to make himself become invisible by means of a special machine created by his number one henchman, Lucifer. In reality The Ghost is a member of a crime-fighting committee known as the Council of Eight. Because the Council has eliminated his brother, "Rackets" Reagan, The Ghost has taken revenge by eliminating three of the Council's members and vows to destroy the others as well. As the serial progresses the Council is further decimated until we finally learn the identity of The Ghost in Chapter Fifteen. (All four Tracy serials, by the way, were made up of fifteen episodes each.) If you were reasonably smart you could pick out The Ghost in the very first chapter because this was one of those rare exceptions where the actual suspect's voice was used. In the case of most serials another actor's voice was usually dubbed in to confuse the audience and prevent them from guessing the truth too soon. Other examples of mystery men using their own voices are The Octopus in *The Spider's Web* and Pegleg in *Overland With Kit Carson. Dick Tracy vs. Crime, Inc.* had some interesting chapter endings. One chapter found Tracy trapped in a blazing inferno which director William Witney recalls nearly got completely out of control. (A similar fire staged a year earlier by Witney for *Adventures of Red Ryder did* go out of control and nearly burned down a soundstage.) Another blazing ending found Tracy lying on a conveyor belt that was slowly drawing him into an open-air incin-erator. In addition to nearly being cremated, Tracy was nearly killed in boat and plane crashes, explosions, and by nearly falling into a bottomless pit.

The finale of *Dick Tracy vs. Crime, Inc.* is memorable. Tracy discovers that the only way to uncover The Ghost is by luring him into a room in which he has placed an infra-red light bulb. This bulb, when lit, will reverse the polarity of the room causing The Ghost to appear in bold relief. The trick works (accomplished simply by printing the entire sequence on negative film stock) and a terrific fight ensues. Tracy follows The Ghost to a power plant where the villain tries to escape by crossing high tension wires. A guard at the plant who is freed from his bonds turns on the power switch and we see the invisible form of The Ghost burst into flames and plummet to the ground. Could any kid ever forget a scene like that?

With the completion of this fourth serial, Ralph Byrd thought he was at last finished with Tracy, but such was not to be the case. A few years later RKO-Radio Pictures began a series of four Tracy features. The first two starred the character actor Morgan Conway as the comic strip sleuth, but were not successful and Byrd was brought in to do the remaining two films.

Finale? Not quite. Television was on the horizon and in the flurry to do series shows like *The Lone Ranger, Sky King* and *The Cisco Kid,* it was natural to do a series featuring Tracy and many of his comic strip pals (like Vitamin Flintheart and Gravel Gertie). Once again Byrd was selected to play the lead. The series was a disaster. Shortly afterwards Ralph Byrd died, and with him the serial character of Dick Tracy also disappeared.

We should mention in passing that Tracy was also done as an animated cartoon strip for television, but it was strictly juvenile in conception and unworthy of a character who had developed such a loyal and dedicated following over the years.

REPUBLIC PICTURES presents

DICK TRACY

Based on cartoon strip
by CHESTER GOULD

Episode I
The SPIDER
STRIKES

with
RALPH BYRD
KAY HUGHES
Smiley BURNETTE
LEE VAN ATTA

Directed by RAY TAYLOR
and ALAN JAMES
Produced by
NAT LEVINE

A
REPUBLIC
SERIAL

in
15
Action
EPISODES

Above, Ralph Byrd and Fred Hamilton disguise themselves as cameramen in order to get a clue to The Spider's whereabouts in *Dick Tracy* (Republic, 1937).

Below, The cast of *Dick Tracy* (Republic, 1937) featured Smiley Burnette, Kay Hughes, Fred Hamilton, Ralph Byrd and Lee Van Atta.

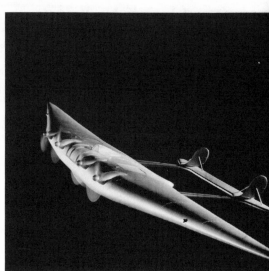

Left, More important than actors in most Republic serials were the special effects created to make spectacular cliffhanger endings. Here Howard Lydecker tests the path a miniature car will take. The secret of Republic's miniatures was that they were meticulously scaled relatively large and were photographed outdoors using natural light.

Below, Another shot of the miniature of The Wing used in *Dick Tracy* (Republic, 1937).

Bottom, Howard and Theodore Lydecker suspend the miniature aircraft, The Wing, used in *Dick Tracy* (Republic, 1937) and in *Fighting Devil Dogs.*

Above, Dick Tracy couldn't really fly too far in this plane mock-up against a blank rear projection screen. An unedited still from *Dick Tracy Returns* (Republic, 1938).

Left, Pitting himself against Dick Tracy was The Spider (also called The Lame One) and his minions (Harrison Greene and John Piccori) in *Dick Tracy* (Republic, 1937).

Below, Young David Sharpe's law enforcement career is ended when The Kid, one of Pa Stark's boys, guns him down. Junior (Jerry Tucker) and Dick (Ralph Byrd) help Sharpe as best they can in *Dick Tracy Returns* (Republic, 1938).

Above, When his air is cut off, Tracy (Ralph Bryd) makes a rapid dash for safety in *Dick Tracy's G-Men* (Republic, 1939).

Left, You can bet anything that after this setup Tracy (Ralph Byrd) will wind up under those timbers at the end of a chapter of *Dick Tracy's G-Men* (Republic, 1939).

Below, As the thirties ended, less and less exterior location work was done on the serials like this dam sequence for *Dick Tracy's G-Men* (Republic, 1939) with Ralph Byrd and Ted Pearson.

Above, Ralph Byrd and Ted Pearson look for some incriminating evidence while Bud Geary gives them the once-over in *Dick Tracy's G-Men* (Republic, 1939).

Left, Even for Ralph Byrd in *Dick Tracy vs. Crime, Inc.* (Republic, 1941), rescuing Jan Wiley from a blazing inferno can be exhausting work.

Below, Ralph Byrd as Dick Tracy in *Dick Tracy vs. Crime, Inc.* (Republic, 1941).

46

Above left, In a final blaze of glory, Ralph Byrd completes the fourth and last of the Dick Tracy serials, *Dick Tracy vs. Crime, Inc.* (Republic, 1941).

Right, Tracy and the sign are headed for a perilous plunge in *Dick Tracy vs. Crime, Inc.* (Republic, 1941).

Below, Tracy leaps from the truck only seconds before the deadly device explodes in *Dick Tracy vs. Crime, Inc.* (Republic, 1941).

NOTHING SEEMED TO thrill audiences quite as much as the image of a masked rider thundering across the plains to mete out justice to those who had transgressed. What matter if the entire concept of vigilante justice was morally wrong, as long as it was exciting and the bad guys wound up dead? These avenging horsemen were daring, colorful extensions of our own desires to see right triumph over wrong, and the boldest rider of them all was the legendary Zorro.

Created by Johnston McCulley for his story, *The Curse of Capistrano,* which appeared in installments in the 1919 *All-Story* pulp magazine, Zorro travelled through early California righting wrongs done to the peasants by an unscrupulous Governor. In 1920 Douglas Fairbanks, Sr. created a sensation in an adaptation called *The Mark of Zorro.* Two decades later, Tyrone Power made a vastly inferior sound remake of the tale. The character also appeared in Republic's first color film, the 1937 *The Bold Caballero,* with Robert Livingston as the devil-may-care lead.

Zorro was a character born for serial treatment and Republic wasted little time in bringing in a dashing young cabaret entertainer named John Carroll to wear the mask in the twelve-chapter *Zorro Rides Again* (1937). Carroll played James Vega, a great-grandson of the original Don Diego Vega, in a move to update the character so that trains, trucks and other modern conveyances could be utilized. The simple plot had villains Richard Alexander and Noah Beery, Sr. trying to thwart the legitimate interests of the California-Yucatan Railroad. It was not an easy serial to make. Carroll, new to films and difficult to work with, caused director William Witney to finally lay down the law. Either Carroll got down to work, or Witney would take him off the film. The actor relented and turned in a first-rate job as he sang (not much, only a couple of choruses of a special song written for the film) and fought his way to Chapter Twelve. One interesting sidelight was in the casting of Noah Beery, Sr. His role and salary had been much heralded, but when he showed up for work, all his scenes were shot in a single day. The writers on *Zorro Rides Again* used traditional chapter endings such as having Zorro get his boot stuck between tracks as a train

roared closer or Zorro trapped in a flaming building, as well as an exceptional climax which found our hero plummeting to almost certain death down a construction tramway of a dam. Heady stuff, indeed.

Although many people prefer *Zorro Rides Again,* most serial devotees believe that *Zorro's Fighting Legion,* produced in 1939, is really the best of all the Zorro serials. Reed Hadley, (later to do many voice-over narrations for such 20th Century-Fox features as *The House on 92nd Street)* was a perfect choice to play the dual role of the foppish Diego Vega and the dashing Zorro. Whereas *Zorro Rides Again* was a straight action film, *Zorro's Fighting Legion* added an element of mystery. A colorful reincarnation of a Yaqui god called Don Del Oro was inciting the natives to rebellion in order to grab California for his own purposes. Don Del Oro was really one of several suspect council members. Zorro, equally adept with guns or whip, survived avalanches, explosions, flooded tunnels and collapsing bridges in order to reveal Don Del Oro's real identity. Justice is administered on the spot as the natives backed the culprit into certain death in a fiery pit. Adding to the overall superiority of *Zorro's Fighting Legion* was an exceptionally original and exciting score by William Lava and Cy Feuer. One of the real assets of most Republic serials was the use of pulse-pounding music which made the action often seem a great deal better than it actually was. Yakima Canutt, who had been Carroll's stunt double in the previous serial, did similar duty here with an occasional assist from Ted Mapes and the rest of the Republic stunt staff.

Five years passed before another Zorro serial would be made, but this time it would be in name only. In *Zorro's Black Whip* the only mention of Zorro was in the film's title. Linda Stirling, Republic's then-current serial queen, portrayed a character called The Whip, having assumed the role from her brother who was killed in Chapter One. Around for physical and moral support was George J. Lewis portraying a leading man in a welcome change of pace from his usual role as a villain. Much as Republic wanted to give women bigger roles, they still needed a man to do all the fisticuffs required to suit action fans. Francis MacDonald was the behind-the-scenes despot who was

Left, Equally adept with either whip or gun, John Carroll as Zorro returns to the screen in *Zorro Rides Again* (Republic, 1937).

trying to capture the entire territory for himself, but wound up being trampled to death by The Whip's horse at film's end. Although *Zorro's Black Whip* had all the necessary ingredients, the end result was merely a routine Western serial enlivened only by the excellent performances of Stirling and Lewis.

In *Son of Zorro* we return to a storyline encompassing a mystery angle once again as a mysterious "Chief" tried to gain control of (again) all the territory in the region. Behind the mask this time around was tall, good-looking George Turner. Turner, a man who had some boxing experience, quickly got into trouble with the Republic stunt team when he tried to throw more realistic-looking punches. Stuntmen are a hearty breed, however, and George was quickly shown the error of his ways and performed the required tasks as outlined. Although most of the footage was original, on occasion some stock footage from earlier serials like *Zorro's Black Whip* and *Daredevils of the West* was used for chapter endings. Peggy Stewart, one of Republic's most durable B-Western leading ladies, had the co-starring role. How Turner became Zorro was explained away by the simple line that "Zorro was an ancestor on my mother's side" in Chapter One. Ah, well, it was 1947 and near the end of the trail for our masked defender.

Republic's final entry in the series was the 1949 *Ghost of Zorro* with popular Clayton Moore now riding the trail to try and get a telegraph line completed before Gene Roth and his ruthless gang destroy everything in sight. Moore was one of Republic's best-liked leading men as far as audiences were concerned. He rode well, had a pleasant speaking voice and could effectively handle the action sequences in close-ups. This was the same year that Moore began his long tenure as television's Lone Ranger, a role he seemed born to assume even though it would hinder his future roles as an actor.

In the 1950's when Walt Disney's *Zorro* television series was going full steam, Republic, ever on the alert, re-edited *Zorro Rides Again* and *Ghost of Zorro* into two feature versions which played as a dual bill in the hopes of grabbing attention from the television faithful.

Although the Zorro series had really called it a day with *Ghost of Zorro*, Republic did make two additional serials in which the leading characters dressed in a Zorro outfit in order to utilize stock footage from the earlier quality productions in these last-ditch efforts. The first of these was the 1951 *Don Daredevil Rides Again* featuring Ken Curtis (who became very well known for his continuing role as Festus in the television series, *Gunsmoke).* In this adventure our masked hero was out to break up a landgrab scheme hatched by veteran badman Roy Barcroft. Three years later Richard Simmons was the masked man for whom they were matching stock shots in *Man With the Steel Whip.* Mauritz Hugo found out that there was a rich vein of gold on some Indian territory and it took Simmons twelve chapters to show him the error of his ways.

Although technically it wasn't a Zorro serial, mention should be made of Republic's 1936 production of *The Vigilantes Are Coming.* In this early effort, Robert Livingston portrayed a masked rider called The Eagle who eventually succeeded in thwarting the attempt of Fred Kohler to establish himself as the permanent dictator of early California. In a strange plot twist Kohler enlists the aid of Russian cossacks to help him in his mad quest. Livingston, in his unmasked personality, assumes an air of complacent innocence as he pretends to be a church organist. Yakima Canutt delivers one of the great quotable serial lines when, looking at Livingston, he proclaims that "anyone who plays the organ can't be any good." We knew something he didn't!

The Zorro character, whether officially sanctioned or not, has appeared in numerous slipshod foreign productions that deserve little mention. In the fifties Walt Disney brought the character to television in a regular series which, for some still unexplained reason, was shot in glorious black and white when almost everything else the studio did for television was done in color. William Lava, who almost twenty years earlier had done such an outstanding score for *Zorro's Fighting Legion,* wrote the background music for this new series which, sad to say, had little of the flavor of the original.

Will Zorro make a comeback? Only time will tell, but no doubt someone is waiting in the wings to wear the mask of justice once again. Perhaps it is a relative to whom Zorro was an ancestor on his grand-uncle's side. And then again, perhaps not.

John Carroll as Zorro's alter-ego James Vega in *Zorro Rides Again* (Republic, 1937).

John Carroll as Zorro gets things under control in *Zorro Rides Again* (Republic, 1937).

Left, Ever vigilant, John Carroll as Zorro keeps his eye on El Lobo and his men in *Zorro Rides Again* (Republic, 1937).

Left, Reed Hadley as Zorro escapes the deadly crushing walls by lifting a rock from the floor in *Zorro's Fighting Legion* (Republic, 1939).

Right, The best of all the serial Zorros, Reed Hadley in *Zorro's Fighting Legion* (Republic, 1939).

Above, One of the contributing factors to the success of *Zorro's Fighting Legion* was an original music score composed by William Lava, shown here in a 1946 portrait. He also scored *Daredevils of the Red Circle* and other favorites.

Below, When Francisco (Guy D'Ennery) is mortally wounded, Zorro (Reed Hadley) and Ramon (William Corson) swear to avenge his death in *Zorro's Fighting Legion* (Republic, 1939).

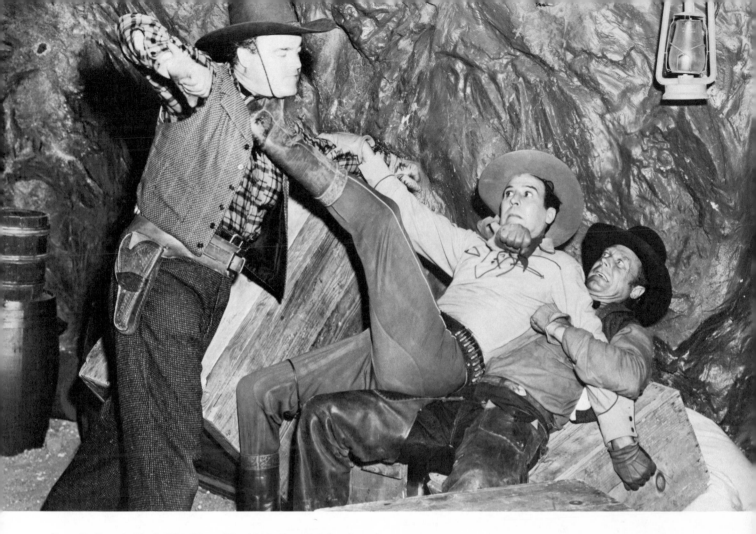

Above, In *Zorro's Black Whip* (Republic, 1944) George J. Lewis took on all comers, as in this matchup with John Merton and Hal Taliaferro.

Below, Although the title of the film was *Zorro's Black Whip* (Republic, 1944), Linda Stirling was merely referred to as The Whip.

Right, Linda Stirling and George J. Lewis in *Zorro's Black Whip* (Republic, 1944). George has temporarily assumed The Whip's identity to save Linda's life.

Above, George Turner as Zorro comes to the aid of Peggy Stewart in *Son of Zorro* (Republic, 1947).

Left, Roy Barcroft has George Turner completely at his mercy (for the time being) in *Son of Zorro* (Republic, 1947).

Right, Clayton Moore as Zorro had the assistance of Pamela Blake in *Ghost of Zorro* (Republic, 1949).

Below, In *Ghost of Zorro* (Republic, 1949) Clayton Moore fights off stunt ace Dale Van Sickel.

Right, Utilizing stock footage from earlier efforts, Ken Curtis was the masked hero of *Don Daredevil Rides Again* (Republic, 1951). This scene shows him as Lee Hadley.

Below, George J. Lewis was Clayton Moore's sidekick in *Ghost of Zorro* (Republic, 1949).

Far right, Dressed in Zorro-like garb, Ken Curtis is now the Don in *Don Daredevil Rides Again* (Republic, 1951).

58

In this production shot Don Daredevil (Ken Curtis) fights in a burning wagon in front of a process screen while two prop men keep the wheels turning in *Don Daredevil Rides Again* (Republic, 1951).

Left, Richard Simmons as El Latigo in *Man with the Steel Whip* (Republic, 1954).

Below, In a final fling at imitating Zorro, Richard Simmons became El Latigo and rode with Barbara Bestar to avenge injustice in *Man with the Steel Whip* (Republic, 1954).

6 THE COMICS COME TO LIFE

IN THE MID-THIRTIES, the appeal of the serials had begun to diminish when suddenly the newspaper comic strip burst onto the pop culture scene with a flood of new and colorful heroes to excite young fans. Reading the Sunday and daily strips became an enjoyable ritual for young and old alike. The shrewd serial producers quickly saw the commercial advantage in transferring these new idols to the screen and before long Saturday afternoon business was booming once again.

Universal, whose early talkie serials lacked any genuine creativity, was the first to utilize the services of a pen and ink hero when it brought Tailspin Tommy to the screen in two aerial adventures. Although the characters themselves were interesting enough, both *Tailspin Tommy* and *Tailspin Tommy in the Great Air Mystery* suffered from a common studio fault: the overuse of stock footage from earlier features. In the case of these films it was the repeated dogfights and action sequences from *Hell's Angels,* (among others) that gave the films a disjointed, patchwork look that prevented a sense of complete enjoyment. However, things took a turn for the better in 1936 when Universal bought the rights to a whole package of strips owned by King Features Syndicate. Heading the list was an Alex Raymond character whose Sunday exploits had captured the imagination of the world—Flash Gordon. The studio spent a great deal of money in transferring *Flash Gordon* to the screen, and their choice of Buster Crabbe to play the leading role was a rare touch of studio genius. For all its imaginative trappings, the serial itself has many faults, including frequent bad acting in supporting roles, cheap-looking miniatures, and a dullness of pace that makes the serial boring at times. But you can't argue with success. *Flash Gordon* was to be the studio's most popular serial, and continued showings on television testify to its nostalgic appeal. Buoyed by the film's profits, two sequels were filmed: *Flash Gordon's Trip to Mars* and *Flash Gordon Conquers the Universe.* Both were better technically; yet neither matched the color and excitement of the original.

Also in the King Features package was *Tim Tyler's Luck,* which found young Frankie Thomas, as Tim, after the notorious Spider Webb and his gang who were traveling through the jungle in an armor-plated conveyance called a "jungle cruiser"; *Ace Drummond,* with John King after a hidden villain called The Dragon in adventures inspired by the Eddie Rickenbacker strip; *Secret Agent X-9,* with Scott Kolk as another Alex Raymond creation (another version of *Secret Agent X-9* was made in 1945 with Lloyd Bridges fighting Axis agents); *Jungle Jim,* with Grant Withers after a fortune and the mysterious enemy called The Cobra: *Radio Patrol,* with Grant Withers trying to solve a strange murder centered around the fight for control of a formula to create "flexible steel"; and, finally, *Red Barry,* with Buster Crabbe in an inferior mish-mash of intrigue in a Chinatown setting. Universal's remaining comic strip adaptations consisted of two above-average naval adventures (*Don Winslow of the Navy* and *Don Winslow of the Coast Guard* in which the intrepid hero battled The Scorpion), *Buck Rogers* (an attempt that failed, even with Buster Crabbe starring, to duplicate *Flash Gordon's* success) and *Adventures of Smilin' Jack* (which pitted young Tom Brown, as Jack, against an espionage ring). In all, Universal made sixteen serials using newspaper favorites.

Giving Universal a good run for its money was Columbia Pictures with fifteen serial adaptations. Two King Features properties which had escaped Universal's pact were *Mandrake, the Magician* and *Terry and the Pirates.* On screen, the former featured Warren Hull as the master magician fighting a masked villain called The Wasp; the latter starred young William Tracy as Terry Lee trying to uncover a lost civilization. In 1943 the studio brought *Batman* to the screen in an outlandish, comic-laden adventure which found Lewis Wilson playing the cowled crusader and doing battle with J. Carrol Naish as a leering and laughable Japanese agent. A sequel, *Batman and Robin,* was made six years later with Robert Lowery in the lead and was much more exciting, even though Lowery had constant trouble trying to see through his eye slits in a poorly-fitting costume. Tom Tyler cut a striking figure in the title role of *The Phantom,* but the serial itself was a meaningless fiasco. One good chapter ending found The Phantom trapped under a huge spear-lined gate which was slowly descending upon him. Women got a small break

Left, Tom Tyler was a perfect choice to portray the hero of Republic's best-remembered serial, *Adventures of Captain Marvel* (Republic, 1941).

when *Brenda Starr, Reporter,* with Joan Woodbury in the title role, made the transition from paper to screen. Brenda was after a stolen satchel full of money which, with the aid of her police lieutenant pal (Kane Richmond), she finally recovered. Other Columbia favorites included: *The Vigilante,* with Ralph Byrd taking time off from his Dick Tracy portrayals to locate a valuable string of pearls; *Brick Bradford,* with veteran serial star Kane Richmond in an adventure that started out with great science-fiction possibilities, but wound up almost as a straight Western-type adventure; *Tex Granger,* with Robert Kellard in routine Western fare; *Congo Bill,* starring Don McGuire in a routine jungle epic that looked as though it had been filmed in someone's backyard; *Bruce Gentry,* with Tom Neal trying to stop some comically-animated "flying discs" from destroying key strategic targets; *Blackhawk,* starring a very capable Kirk Alyn in an exciting adventure dealing with the capture of a sabotage ring and, to round out the list, an awful Buster Crabbe serial, *King of the Congo,* based on the character Thunda. Columbia's biggest serial successes based on artists' creations were *Superman* and *Atom Man vs. Superman.* With Kirk Alyn as "The Man of Steel," these two serials played many of the country's "A" theaters. (Unlike most serial adventures, which played the usual "scratch houses.") Although both serials were done with humor, the fans loved them and flocked to see the sepia-toned (used as an advertising gimmick) tales of America's best-known superhero.

Republic, the best of the serial-producing companies, realized early on that it was much cheaper to develop its own characters than to pay rights and get into legal hassles with stubborn copyright owners. They did, however, devote ten of their sixty-six productions to fictional newspaper heroes, and in each case the studio scored a commercial and critical bulls-eye. Four of these adventures featured popular Ralph Byrd as the celebrated detective, Dick Tracy. As the scripts progressed with *Dick Tracy, Dick Tracy Returns, Dick Tracy's G-Men* and *Dick Tracy vs. Crime, Inc.,* production quality got better and better. Inventive plots, fine location shooting and excellent casting in supporting roles made the Tracy adventures a continuing joy to behold. Fred Harman's popular Western strip was given cinema treatment in *Adventures of Red Ryder.* Star Donald Barry hated playing the role because he felt he was terribly miscast, but the serial made him a star. Later, when he went on to star in dozens of B-Western features, most fans remembered him with the name he quickly acquired, Don "Red" Barry. Allan Lane became popular at Republic as a B-Western star in later years, but his first experiences with quality action fare were in *King of the Royal Mounted* and *King of the Mounties,* two colorful tales which found our hero pitted against enemy agents threatening our northern neighbors. Republic had tried to get the rights to *Superman* as early as 1940, but when they failed they turned to another superhero who at one time was even more popular than The Man of Steel—Captain Marvel. Tom Tyler was a perfect choice to play the title role in *Adventures of Captain Marvel,* thwarting the evil schemes of The Scorpion who was out to control a devilish device with which he could rule the world. With superb special effects, particularly in the well-staged flying sequences, *Adventures of Captain Marvel* has become Republic's favorite and most respected serial. When the studio acquired rights to Captain Marvel from Fawcett Publications, Republic also received the right to transfer *Spy Smasher* to celluloid. In *Spy Smasher* Kane Richmond played a dual role as the costumed hero and his twin brother who were both on the trail of a Nazi agent known as The Mask. With David Sharpe doing the stunt work, *Spy Smasher* was another thrill-laden adventure that did exceedingly well at the box office. When Republic brought *Captain America* to the screen, gone were Bucky, his young companion, his famous shield and the wings adorning his mask. Because of the studio's method of treating fight sequences, these three items featured in the comic strip were deemed a hindrance, so they were simply dropped. *Captain America,* with Dick Purcell portraying the lead, was the studio's most expensive serial production, costing almost $223,000 (about half the cost of a single hour-long television show today). Crammed with action and explosive visual effects created by the Lydecker brothers, *Captain America* was a most satisfying serial. It also was the final comic strip character that Republic would adapt to the screen, preferring original studio creations for the remaining twelve years of its serial production.

Above, Noel Neill and Tommy Bond look crestfallen as George Meeker and Carol Forman smirk over the prostrate form of Kirk Alyn as The Man of Steel, *Superman* (Columbia, 1948).

Right, Kirk Alyn takes to the air again in *Atom Man vs. Superman* (Columbia, 1950).

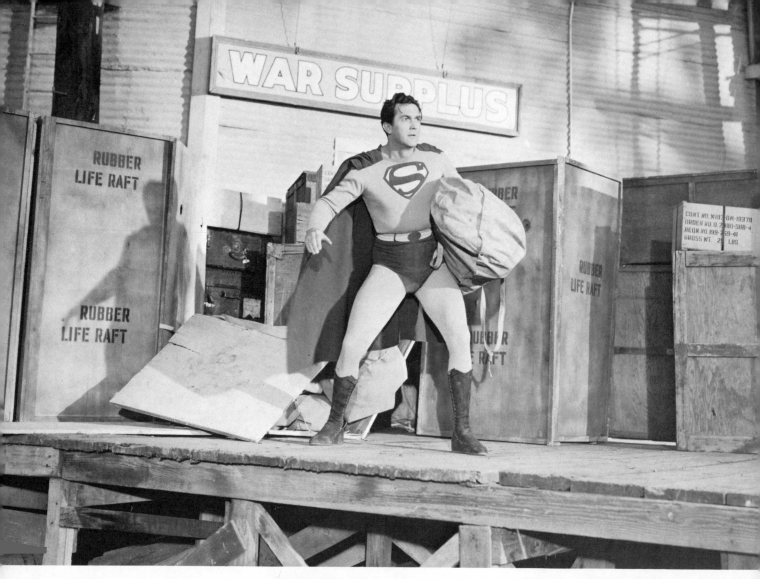

Above, Kirk Alyn imbued Superman with a sense of humor in *Atom Man vs. Superman* (Columbia, 1950).

Right, Aiding Tom Tyler in *The Phantom* (Columbia, 1943) were Jeanne Bates and Frank Shannon (famous for his role as Dr. Zarkov in the three Flash Gordon serials).

Below, Another role tailor-made for Tom Tyler was *The Phantom* (Columbia, 1943). Ace, the Wonder Dog, played Devil. That's John S. Bagni on the right.

Far left, A publicity shot for *Adventures of Captain Marvel* (Republic, 1941) found Tom Tyler giving a super leap.

Left, Judy Canova, one of Republic's hottest stars, dropped by for a little photo session during the making of *Adventures of Captain Marvel* (Republic, 1941) to kid with Tom Tyler.

Below, Raymond Hatton was Malay Mike and Betty Jane Rhodes the Lion Goddess in *Jungle Jim* (Universal, 1937), the title role being played by Grant Withers.

Right, Kirk Alyn was an excellent choice to play *Blackhawk* (Columbia, 1952) and get away from his Superman typecasting.

Here are four typical Columbia serial chapter endings, this time appearing in *Brick Bradford* (Columbia, 1947). In scene one *(top left)* Kane Richmond and Rick Vallin are trapped by an electrical death ray. Scene two *(bottom left)* finds Kane Richmond lying in the path of deadly acid. In scene three *(top right)* Richmond, Vallin and Linda Johnson find themselves being frozen to death by strange vapors. Finally, *(bottom right)* Richmond and Vallin find themselves being burned at the stake.

71

Left, Allen Jung was Connie, William Tracy, Terry, and Granville Owen, Pat Ryan in the film version of the popular strip, *Terry and the Pirates* (Columbia, 1940).

Below, A disguised John King rescues Chester Gan from the closing walls in *Ace Drummond* (Universal, 1936).

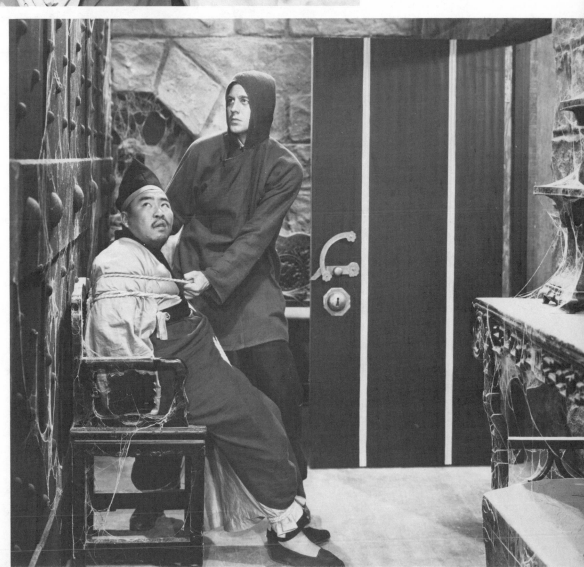

Right, Kane Richmond as *Spy Smasher* (Republic, 1942) stops a descending elevator by jamming his gun into the gears.

Below, Tom Brown looks like he's in a tough predicament in *Adventures of Smilin' Jack* (Universal, 1943).

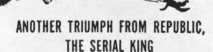

Left, Kay Aldridge as Nyoka inspired a comic strip after the success of *Perils of Nyoka* (Republic, 1942). Fang was played by Ace, the Wonder Dog.

Above, Maurice Murphy and Patricia Farr kept the action moving in *Tailspin Tommy* (Universal, 1934).

Right, A year later Clark Williams and Noah Beery, Jr. brought the flying ace back in *Tailspin Tommy in the Great Air Mystery* (Universal, 1935).

Above, Allan Lane appears to be facing an uncertain future in *King of the Royal Mounted* (Republic, 1940).

Left, One of the chapter endings of *Congo Bill* (Columbia, 1948) found Don McGuire caught in these grinding gears.

Right, Although he disliked playing the role, *Adventures of Red Ryder* (Republic, 1940) made Don "Red" Barry a star.

Tim Tyler's Luck (Universal, 1937) had an excellent cast featuring William Benedict, Frankie Thomas as Tim, Frances Robinson and durable Jack Mulhall.

Above, Dick Purcell as *Captain America* (Republic, 1944) escapes from a generator room before a million volts of electricity can destroy him.

Above, In *Radio Patrol* (Universal, 1937) Grant Withers was Pat O'Hara and Catherine Hughes his comforting lady companion.

Right, Taking a vacation from playing Dick Tracy, Ralph Byrd portrayed another comic strip favorite, *The Vigilante* (Columbia, 1947).

Far right, Warren Hull made an impressive-looking *Mandrake, the Magician* (Columbia, 1939).

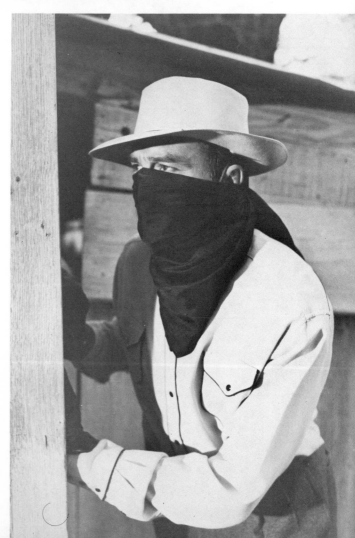

Left, It took six years to bring *Batman and Robin* (Columbia, 1949) to the screen again, this time in the persons of Robert Lowery and John Duncan.

Top right, Douglas Croft as Robin and Lewis Wilson as Batman ponder a complex problem in *Batman* (Columbia, 1943).

Bottom right, The evil Daka, portrayed by J. Carrol Naish, plans to convert Lewis Wilson into a zombie in *Batman* (Columbia, 1943).

Left, The popular female comic strip, *Brenda Starr, Reporter* (Columbia, 1945) was given life by Joan Woodbury. Brenda was assisted for the rough stuff by Kane Richmond as Lt. Larry Farrel.

Below, Tom Neal as *Bruce Gentry* (Columbia, 1949) finally unmasks Forrest Taylor as the unknown villain, The Recorder. Forrest Taylor's voice was used for several Columbia masked villains including The Skull in *Deadwood Dick.*

Above, The first version of *Secret Agent X-9* (Universal, 1937) found Scott Kolk portraying the hero who got the goods on the mysterious Henry Brandon.

Right, Robert Kellard was an ingratiating *Tex Granger* (Columbia, 1948), with a lot of help from Peggy Stewart.

Z PULP MAGAZINE AND RADIO FAVORITES

WHILE THE COMIC PAGES supplied a collection of colorful heroes designed to satisfy the adventurous spirit of American youth, some of the most exciting and durable characters of the day found their origins in two other popular culture media—radio and the pulps. Unlike the drawn strips, radio and pulp magazines offered the individual a chance to use his own imagination in creating visual representations of his favorite crime fighters. Captain Midnight could be tall, short, fat, thin, white, black or any combination desired to suit personal tastes. Unfortunately, when these same ethereal images found themselves being transferred to the screen, the results were often disappointing.

When The Shadow announced at the beginning of each broadcast, "Who knows what evil lurks in the hearts of Men? The Shadow knows . . . "—we knew that for the next thirty minutes we were going to hear a wild adventure that could deal with anything from zombies coming back to life to diabolical scientists bent on destroying the entire world. When Columbia Pictures brought *The Shadow* to the screen all we saw was Victor Jory wearing a cap and mask and engaging in a long series of routine fights and chases that any normal hero could undertake with ease. Far from being able to "cloud men's minds so they cannot see him," the cinema Shadow spent most of his time being trapped in a series of explosions and escaping by simply pushing aside the tons of debris that would have crushed the average man. Jory, a versatile actor who spent most of his time playing villains in Westerns, not only played The Shadow and his everyday role as Lamont Cranston, but frequently put on a ludicrous oriental make-up to play a character called Lin Chang. In this triple masquerade he sought to uncover the mysterious Black Tiger, an underworld czar with mad ambitions. Too often comedy got in the way of the action when, for example, bad guy Charles King announces to his gang, "I had him (The Shadow) right where I wanted him and then everything went black," whereupon he staggers around like a Keystone Kop and then falls backward over a hedge. This kind of stuff was for two-reel comedies, not serials.

Captain Midnight didn't fare much better. For those of us who couldn't wait to get our Secret Squadron Decoder Badge and who sat breathlessly each day waiting to decode the secret message delivered at the end of each program, Columbia's *Captain Midnight* was a disappointment. Again, comedy was the main problem. Dave O'Brien, a likeable actor and stuntman who later appeared in a whole series of Pete Smith shorts as an accident-prone bungler, looked great as the Captain. However, his nemesis, Ivan Shark (played broadly by James Craven who specialized in this type of villainous role at Columbia) was constantly berating his underlings to the point of absurdity as they failed to stop Midnight from interfering with their plans to wreak havoc on defense industries.

On radio, "Gang Busters" was a routine cops and robbers program showing how law enforcement officials brought various criminals to justice. Supposedly based on real-life cases, each show ended with a description of an actual wanted fugitive and listeners were advised to contact the F.B.I. or other law enforcement agency if they had any pertinent information. When *Gang Busters* was put on celluloid it contained a plot more suitable for a character like The Shadow. Ralph Morgan was the head of an organization called "The League of Murdered Men" supposedly made up of criminals who had been executed and then were brought back to life. Hero Kent Taylor finally broke up the gang and Morgan was killed by a speeding subway train as he tried to escape through a secret exit. The serial was good, imaginative fun, but hardly representative of the radio show it was based on.

The most durable of all adventure radio programs was "The Lone Ranger". The exciting tales of a sole Texas Ranger who had escaped a death trap and then vowed to fight injustice along with his horse, Silver, and his faithful Indian companion, Tonto, were listened to by loyal followers for more than two decades. Republic Pictures brought the character to the screen in 1938, but with some changes bordering on the extreme. Instead of letting the viewer know right off who the Ranger was, we were given five suspects (Lee Powell, George Letz [later Montgomery], Herman Brix [later Bruce Bennett], Hal Taliaferro [formerly Wally Wales], and Lane Chandler) and were forced to play a guessing game for fifteen episodes as the suspects were killed off one by one. Excitingly filmed with

Left, Victor Jory, or more likely his stunt double, in *The Shadow* (Columbia, 1940), based on the popular radio and pulp character.

customary Republic skill, inasmuch as B-Westerns were a studio staple, the negatives of *The Lone Ranger* and its sequel, *The Lone Ranger Rides Again,* appear to have vanished completely. Only within the last few years have a few isolated prints with Spanish subtitles appeared. The disappearance of those negatives is really a more intriguing mystery than most serial plots could conspire to create.

With the enthusiastic response of audiences evident, Republic knew it had a winner in *The Lone Ranger* and a year later brought out its sequel, starring personable Robert Livingston as the "Masked Rider of the Plains." This time there was no mystery, only a straightforward action tale, occasionally spiced with humor, photographed with the flavor of Republic's Three Mesquiteer films. All things considered, The Lone Ranger came off pretty well in relation to other heroes making the transition from radio to screen.

George W. Trendle was the man responsible for "The Lone Ranger" radio shows and their success inspired him to create The Green Hornet, who was related by blood to the masked man. The last name of The Lone Ranger and The Green Hornet was Reid, both wore masks and both delivered non-fatal justice to evil doers, the former by means of silver bullets which never killed, only wounded, and the latter with his gas gun which rendered criminals unconscious. Universal brought *The Green Hornet* to the screen in 1940 with Gordon Jones essaying the role. Jones, who was later to become a comic foil for Roy Rogers in features and Abbott and Costello on television, was fine when he played newspaperman Britt Reid, but his voice was not suitable for the Hornet, so the producers flew in Al Hodge (who had played the part on radio) to dub in the Hornet's voice. *The Green Hornet* was one of Universal's better action serials, with the masked crusader combating a criminal gang involved in such varied enterprises as crooked insurance, auto-stealing, and contraband munitions. Like Republic, Universal liked to stick with a winner and within a year *The Green Hornet Strikes Again* was visible on matinee screens. Warren Hull, who went on to become famous on television as the host of "Strike It Rich," gave a much more acceptable performance as The Hornet as he set about the task of breaking up a new gang that was infiltrating most city industries.

Two radio shows that found great followings among younger radio fans were "Jack Armstrong, the All-American Boy" and "Hop Harrigan, Ace of the Airways." Columbia brought both of these characters to cinema life in the middle forties. John Hart seemed a little too old to play the hero from "Hudson High," but as Jack Armstrong he was able to thwart an attempt by a mad scientist (Charles Middleton) to take over the world. William Bakewell as Hop Harrigan fit the role a little more

comfortably as he, too, conquered a lunatic bent on global domination, delightfully conceived by veteran serial heavy John Merton.

Pulp magazines, so named because they were cheaply printed on untrimmed, low-grade paper, usually sold for the low price of a dime or a quarter and featured some exciting characters that also found their way onto the serial screen. Columbia utilized the talents of actor Don Douglas to recreate the Western adventures of *Deadwood Dick* with a good mixture of action and comedy. What matter if the real Deadwood Dick was a black—a little poetic license was in order. Columbia also turned out two serials based on one of pulpdom's most popular heros, The Spider. With his flowing web-insignia cape and mask hiding his identity and his two forty-five automatic pistols dealing death to his enemies, handsome Warren Hull portrayed this colorful character in both *The Spider's Web* and *The Spider Returns.* The former serial truly captured the flavor of the original stories as The Spider uncovered the evil machinations of a mystery man known as The Octopus. By the time the sequel was filmed, Columbia had entered its funny phase and the characters and situations were more geared toward juvenile laughter than thrills as our costumed hero sought out the mysterious Gargoyle, who was a real hoot to watch as he ranted and raved at his underlings. Columbia's attempt to adapt *Chick Carter, Detective,* with an overage Lyle Talbot playing the lead, warrants little notice.

What Jack Armstrong was to one generation, Frank Merriwell was to an earlier one. These athletic adventures created in print by Burt L. Standish served as escapism for many a youth who wished he could play baseball, football or basketball with one-tenth the skill of this fictional he-man. Universal brought the character to the screen in *The Adventures of Frank Merriwell*, with young Don Briggs portraying Merriwell. Train wrecks, bus crashes, falling trees and a variety of other challenges were all met and overcome to the delight of youthful popcorn addicts.

As television was growing in popularity, the serials were already beginning their final phase-out, so only one television series was adapted for the big screen serial format. This was television's popular "Captain Video" which had featured radio's own Green Hornet, Al Hodge, in the title role. Columbia's *Captain Video* gave star Judd Holdren a chance to thwart the diabolical plans of lead villain Gene Roth to conquer the world.

Adapting anything from one media to another is always a risky business at best. However, the studios did their best to give serial fans a faithful portrayal of their favorite characters. If they failed, perhaps the reason was that these bigger-than-life characters were simply too big in the public's imagination to capture on celluloid.

Right, Gordon Jones made an impressive-looking Hornet, but Al Hodge, who portrayed the character on radio, had to fly out to Hollywood to dub his voice in *The Green Hornet* (Universal, 1940).

Below, Character actor Ed Dunn is forced by The Green Hornet, played by Gordon Jones, and Kato, played by Keye Luke, to deliver some valuable evidence in *The Green Hornet* (Universal, 1940).

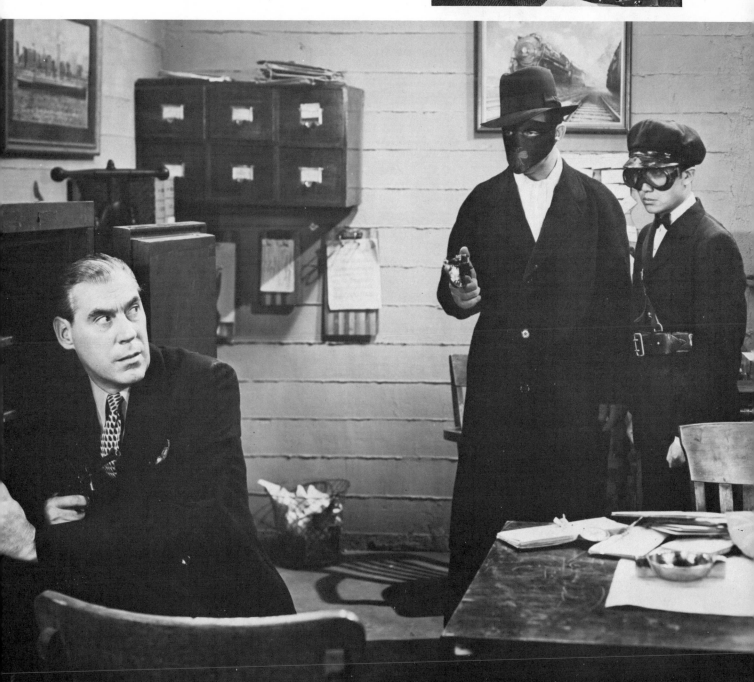

Left, Evans (Alden Chase, left) confronts Axford (Wade Boteler), Lowry (Eddie Acuff) and Britt Reid (Warren Hull) with startling information in *The Green Hornet Strikes Again* (Universal, 1940).

Above, On radio "Gang Busters" was a strait-laced action show dealing with regular criminals. When *Gang Busters* (Universal, 1942) came to the screen it had an unbelievable plot dealing with a supposedly dead group of criminals who formed "The League of Murdered Men." This kind of plot was more in The Shadow's line. In this scene Ralph Morgan, Ralf Harolde and William Haade appear to have the upper hand on hero Kent Taylor.

Right, Universal didn't wait long to bring back the character. Later the same year Warren Hull played The Hornet with Keye Luke again playing Kato. In this scene from *The Green Hornet Strikes Again* (Universal, 1940) Anne Nagel again played the Hornet's right hand girl, Lenore Case, while Warren Hull used the Hornet's famous gas gun.

93

Below, Dave O'Brien, Mary Ainslee and the costumed Warren Hull were hot on the trail of The Gargoyle in *The Spider Returns* (Columbia, 1941).

Right, In a publicity pose, Kenneth Duncan does a little character analysis before undertaking his role of Ram Singh in *The Spider's Web* (Columbia, 1938).

Below, Warren Hull as The Spider was never one to make a subtle entrance, as shown here in Chapter One of *The Spider's Web* (Columbia, 1938).

Top left, Lyle Talbot (left) as *Chick Carter, Detective* (Columbia, 1946) looks to Kermit Maynard for some assistance.

Bottom left, In this chapter ending from *Captain Midnight* (Columbia, 1942), Dave O'Brien is forced into a room which will soon fill with water.

Above, Captain Midnight (Columbia, 1942) gave Dave O'Brien a chance to show off his athletic prowess.

Top left, Except for the fact that the real Deadwood Dick was black, Don Douglas, with the help of Lorna Gray, gave an energetic performance in *Deadwood Dick* (Columbia, 1940).

Bottom left, Veteran director James Horne goes over the script of *Deadwood Dick* (Columbia, 1940).

Above, Don Briggs engaged in boxing, baseball and other sports as well as solving a mystery in *The Adventures of Frank Merriwell* (Universal, 1936).

"THE SHADOW"
HOT FROM RADIO AND MAGAZINE!
with
VICTOR JORY
VEDA ANN BORG • ROGER MOORE • ROBERT FISKE
BASED UPON STORIES PUBLISHED IN "THE SHADOW" MAGAZINE
SCREEN PLAY BY JOSEPH POLAND • NED DANDY • JOSEPH O'DONNELL
Directed by JAMES W. HORNE
A COLUMBIA CHAPTER PLAY

Left, John Hart in the title role of *Jack Armstrong* (Columbia, 1947) is nearly killed in this savage attack.

Below, The only serial to be inspired by a television series was *Captain Video* (Columbia, 1951). Judd Holdren was the Captain and Larry Stewart his Video Ranger.

Above, Director Derwin Abrahams puts Jennifer Holt and William Bakewell in an unusually romantic pose for *Hop Harrigan* (Columbia, 1946). The couple were really man and wife for a time.

Right, Herman Brix is behind the mask this time, and joins Lynn Roberts in going over the shooting script of *The Lone Ranger* (Republic, 1938) with co-director William Witney.

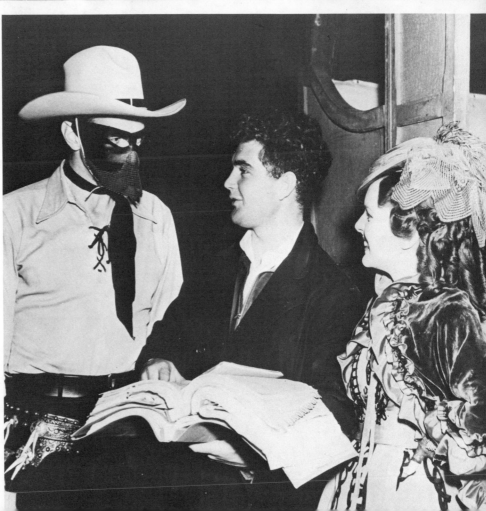

Left, Chief Thundercloud and Lee Powell do a publicity pose for *The Lone Ranger* (Republic, 1938).

Below, Robert Livingston in *The Lone Ranger Rides Again* (Republic, 1939) gets the drop on a cave full of outlaws.

Left, Lee Powell, one of five suspects, turned out to be *The Lone Ranger* (Republic, 1938).

Below, Robert Livingston in a striking portrait used to promote *The Lone Ranger Rides Again* (Republic, 1939). This time there was no mystery, and it seemed that too many people knew who The Lone Ranger was.

THE PREREQUISITES FOR being signed by a studio to star as a serial hero were not at all demanding. If an actor could work fast, was willing to receive little pay, closely resembled a stuntman on the lot who could do his action sequences, and was willing to accept the stigma of working in a product that was considered juvenile pap, he stood a good chance of making the grade in a serial. In spite of these conditions it is surprising how many really competent players turned up rather regularly in these action adventures.

Kane Richmond is probably best remembered for his three Shadow features turned out by Monogram in the mid-forties, but he ranked close to Buster Crabbe in the number of serial appearances made. Beginning in the thirties with *The Adventures of Rex and Rinty*, *The Lost City* (a dreadful serial which even Richmond couldn't save), and a lesser role in *Flash Gordon's Trip to Mars*, the handsome star went on to create superb characterizations in Republic's *Spy Smasher* and *Haunted Harbor* in the early forties. He finished his serial list over at Columbia in less-distinguished performances in *Brenda Starr, Reporter*, and *Jungle Raiders* in 1945 and bade goodbye to the genre with *Brick Bradford* in 1947. Richmond's quiet intensity and determination to do a good job made him one of the all-time favorite action stars.

Clayton Moore also received many critical kudos from young admirers who found him portraying a variety of good and bad guys in serials. Moore showed great promise as a rising young actor in major films like *The Son of Monte Cristo* and *Kit Carson*, in which he had quality supporting roles. However, for some reason he just didn't make the grade and wound up over at Republic doing bit roles. He finally was cast as Kay Aldridge's co-star in the successful *Perils of Nyoka* and things began to look up. Unfortunately, World War II was declared and Clayton served Uncle Sam for the duration. He found himself back at Republic in 1946, cast as a villain in *The Crimson Ghost*. Better things lay ahead, however—Clayton was soon playing the lead in such serials as *Jesse James Rides Again, G-Men Never Forget, Adventures of Frank and Jesse James, Ghost of Zorro* and *Jungle Drums of Africa*. He also made another villainous appearance in Republic's *Radar Men*

from the Moon as well as appearing in Columbia's *Son of Geronimo* and *Gunfighters of the Northwest* in the fifties. As popular as Moore was in the serials, however, his real fame was garnered when he became the Lone Ranger on television. His fine physique and well-modulated voice made him an excellent choice for the role.

Kirk Alyn brought his winning smile and physical presence to a number of exciting serials at both Republic and Columbia. For Republic he starred in *Daughter of Don Q, Federal Agents vs. Underworld, Inc.,* and *Radar Patrol vs. Spy King*. At Columbia he did his most memorable work in *Blackhawk* and as the colorful star of *Superman* and *Atom Man vs. Superman*. Kirk Alyn, like Buster Crabbe, spends a good deal of his time these days attending nostalgia conventions where he is a favorite with fans who revel in his stories about making the serials.

Victor Jory had long-since established himself as an excellent film and stage actor, appearing in many quality productions (including *Gone With the Wind*), so his tour of duty as a matinee star was strictly a lark. In *The Shadow,* Jory was kept in a constant state of anxiety as he kept switching from his role as Lamont Cranston into the mysterious, black-cloaked Shadow, as well as into the Oriental Lin Chang. Jory, with a Fu Manchu-like mustache, almost-buck teeth and over-slanted eyes, made Lin Chang one of the really laughable serial personalities. The likable star was also good for quite a few laughs as he ducked in and out of any number of secret hiding places in *The Green Archer.*

Charles Quigley never achieved any degree of real stardom, but he was a very effective hero in *Daredevils of the Red Circle, The Iron Claw,* and *The Crimson Ghost.* The same is true of veteran Western player Dennis Moore who starred in *The Purple Monster Strikes, Perils of the Wilderness, Raiders of Ghost City,* and *The Master Key.* Moore also holds the dubious distinction of being the star of Universal's last serial, *The Mysterious Mr. M* as well as the star of Columbia's final presentation, *Blazing the Overland Trail.*

Herman Brix (who later changed his name to Bruce Bennett) really made a top-flight Ape Man in *The New Adventures of Tarzan,* and made appearances as star or co-

Left, long before he became The Cisco Kid in films and on television, Duncan Renaldo was the hero's sidekick in many serials. This portrait is from *King of the Texas Rangers* (Republic, 1941).

star in *Shadow of Chinatown, The Lone Ranger, Fighting Devil Dogs, Hawk of the Wilderness* (in which he played his best role as Kioga) and *Daredevils of the Red Circle.* As Bruce Bennett, Brix was one of only a handful of serial players who did major film work. His best-remembered features include roles in *The Treasure of the Sierra Madre* with Humphrey Bogart and *Mildred Pierce* with Joan Crawford.

Veteran B-film player Robert Lowery got a chance to play a costumed hero in *Batman and Robin,* but starred in less flamboyant roles in *Mystery of the River Boat* and *The Monster and the Ape.*

Warren Hull earned everlasting fame with a generation of early television watchers as the host of a mind-bending show called *Strike It Rich* in which people would come before the camera and tell heart-wrenching stories of their personal problems. A telephone called "The Heart Line" was always at the ready to receive calls from benefactors who would call in to offer a job or some other means of help. A decade earlier Hull had been on serial screens as the star of such popular titles as *The Spider's Web, The Spider Returns, The Green Hornet Strikes Again* and *Mandrake, the Magician,* giving a bravado performance in each.

Among other notable performers were: Ralph Byrd in the four Dick Tracy serials as well as *Blake of Scotland Yard, SOS Coast Guard* and *The Vigilante;* Paul Kelly as the Black Commando in *The Secret Code;* Don Terry as Don Winslow in two naval adventures, as well as solving *The Secret of Treasure Island;* Rod Cameron fighting his way through two Republic blockbusters, *G-Men vs. the Black Dragon* and *Secret Service in Darkest Africa;* Dave O'Brien as *Captain Midnight* and the star of the earlier independent, *The Black Coin;* Marshall Reed, who quit playing heavies long enough to star in *Riding with Buffalo Bill;* John Hart in *Jack Armstrong* and *Adventures of Captain Africa* (Hart also played the Lone Ranger for a year on television when star Clayton Moore held out for better money); and last, but certainly not the least, Allan Lane as the hero of *King of the Royal Mounted, King of the Mounties, Daredevils of the West* and *The Tiger Woman.* There are dozens of others, many of whom are mentioned in other sections of this book, but the above seem to have drawn the most favorable audience response.

Mention should also be made of the many supporting players who provided everything from heroic rescues of their top-billed co-stars to simple comedy relief. Long before he became famous as The Cisco Kid, Duncan Renaldo was helping save the heroes of *Zorro Rides Again* (John Carroll), *The Lone Ranger Rides Again* (Robert Livingston), *King of the Texas Rangers* ("Slingin' Sammy" Baugh), *Secret Service in Darkest Africa* (Rod Cameron) and *The Tiger Woman* (Allan Lane). Walter Sande was very capable help in *Don Winslow of the Navy, Don Winslow of the Coast Guard* and *The Iron Claw;* Clancy Cooper did similar duty in *The Secret Code* and *Haunted Harbor.* The times dictated that serial heroes be white, so talented black performers like Snowflake, whose real name was Fred Toones, were relegated to minor roles, providing corny laughs in otherwise excellent serials like *Hawk of the Wilderness* and *Daredevils of the Red Circle.* At least Orientals got a little better break with Keye Luke playing roles in the two Green Hornet serials as well as *Secret Agent X-9* (1945 version), *Adventures of Smilin' Jack* and *Lost City of the Jungle.*

While I have mentioned the better performances, there were a number of rather awful serial performances that do deserve some mention: the four leads (Rod Bacon, Richard Clarke, David Bacon and Bill Healy) who were suspects for being *The Masked Marvel* probably rate our booby prize for bad acting, while following close behind are Mala in *Robinson Crusoe of Clipper Island* and Bill Kennedy in *The Royal Mounted Rides Again.*

The title of "The Last Serial Hero" must be awarded to a fine character actor by the name of Harry Lauter who appeared in Republic's final effort, *King of the Carnival,* as well as *Trader Tom of the China Seas* as the screen's last representative of a vanishing breed—the Saturday Matinee Hero.

Robert Wilcox as The Copperhead seeks out the *Mysterious Doctor Satan* (Republic, 1940) with the aid of Ella Neal.

Kay Aldridge has just missed being speared to death as Kane Richmond comes to the rescue in *Haunted Harbor* (Republic, 1944).

Left, Director William Witney, with hand in back pocket, prepares to shoot a scene with Kane Richmond for *Spy Smasher* (Republic, 1942).

Right, Dennis Moore finds himself in deadly peril in *The Purple Monster Strikes* (Republic, 1945).

Below, The Green Archer (Columbia, 1940) featured this fine cast: Kenneth Duncan, Iris Meredith, Forrest Taylor, Dorothy Fay and Victor Jory.

Clayton Moore and Kay Aldridge made a perfect pair of serial stars in *Perils of Nyoka* (Republic, 1942).

William Benedict was a popular supporting player in *Adventures of Captain Marvel* and *Perils of Nyoka* (Republic, 1942). His monkey friend, Jitters, was played by Professor.

Director Spencer Gordon Bennet (in wide-brimmed hat by camera) and cameraman Bud Thackery (in yachting cap standing by camera) get set to film a scene with Kirk Alyn and Roy Barcroft for *Daughter of Don Q* (Republic, 1946).

Above, Virginia Lindley and Bruce Edwards catch Anthony Warde and Duke Green about to make off with a valuable weapon in *The Black Widow* (Republic, 1947).

Below, A disguised Kirk Alyn and Rosemary LaPlanche have Roy Barcroft and Carol Forman right where they want them in *Federal Agents vs. Underworld, Inc.* (Republic, 1949).

Below, Judd Holdren was Commando Cody in a series of twelve adventures each complete in itself which were released to theaters and to television. The serial *Radar Men from the Moon* introduced the Commando Cody character for the first time.

Left, Don Terry and Walter Miller battle for a fortune in treasure in the last chapter of *The Secret of Treasure Island* (Columbia, 1938).

Below, The cameras get set to shoot a scene with Don Terry (at the door) while other cast members remain seated at the dinner table in *The Secret of Treasure Island* (Columbia, 1938).

113

Left, Marjory Clements and Robert Lowery were the somewhat dazed stars of *Mystery of the River Boat* (Universal, 1944).

Below, Stunt and action star Jack Mahoney starred in *Gunfighters of the Northwest* (Columbia, 1954), a serial that was completely shot on location with no interior sets. With several changes of name, he finally ended up as Jock Mahoney.

Right, Herman Brix came out on top again as Kioga in the *Hawk of the Wilderness* (Republic, 1938).

Above, Herman Brix, Charles Quigley and David Sharpe, the three *Daredevils of the Red Circle* (Republic, 1939) try to capture Stanley Price and almost lose their lives in the attempt.

Right, Many serials had what they called an "economy" chapter in which producers saved a few dollars by recapping earlier action (usually endings from chapters one and two) which was then used as chapter eight or nine. Marten Lamont introduced this recap by relating his story to his superiors via recording in *Federal Operator 99* (Republic, 1945).

Left, Charles Quigley finds, as most heroes do, a way to escape from his bonds in *The Crimson Ghost* (Republic, 1946).

Below, Robert Wilke, left, and Fred Graham capture Dick Purcell in *Captain America* (Republic, 1944). It won't be for long.

Top left, Ray "Crash" Corrigan and C. Montague Shaw attempt to escape by pretending to be Volkite robots in *Undersea Kingdom* (Republic, 1936).

Bottom left, Allan Lane finally uncovers the villainy of Kenne Duncan and Stanley Price in Chapter Eleven of *The Tiger Woman* (Republic, 1944).

Right, Clayton Moore and Ramsay Ames give chase in *G-Men Never Forget* (Republic, 1948).

Below, Linda Stirling and Richard Bailey attempt to outrun rampaging waters that have been unleashed in the tunnel by Captain Mephisto in *Manhunt of Mystery Island* (Republic, 1945).

9 .....AND THE VANQUISHED

MANY OF OUR most colorful serial memories are of the long parade of masked mystery villains like The Scorpion and The Clutching Hand who did battle with our favorite heroes, but there was a much more extensive gallery of quite visible menaces who harbored the same mad dreams of world conquest and financial gain.

Charles Middleton's characterization of Ming the Merciless in *Flash Gordon, Flash Gordon's Trip to Mars* and *Flash Gordon Conquers the Universe* reigns supreme among these serial rogues. Ming was delightful to watch as he continually lusted after beautiful Dale Arden and became more paranoid as each trap he laid for Flash Gordon was skillfully evaded by the blonde hero. With his bald head and Fu Manchu-like mustache, he was the perfect embodiment of what screen fans thought was the ultimate villainy at the time, the so-called "Yellow Peril." Middleton, a character actor with exceptional skill, was regularly cast as the lead heavy in scores of B-Westerns, and he was equally at ease whether playing Ming, chasing after a secret explosive compound in *The Miracle Rider* (with Tom Mix in pursuit), or destroying the properties of a man who had sent him to prison in *Daredevils of the Red Circle*.

Another character actor of some standing who graced the serials was Lionel Atwill, usually associated with his many appearances in horror films like *Mystery of the Wax Museum* and *Son of Frankenstein*. Atwill was at his best as The Scarab in *Captain America*, eliminating his enemies by such devices as gas bombs, poison darts and mummifying gas. He seemed less comfortable in roles like The Baron in *Junior G-Men of the Air* and Alex Morel in *Raiders of Ghost City*. The distinguished actor had almost completed his role in *Lost City of the Jungle* when he succumbed to a heart attack and a stand-in, with his back to the camera and his voice dubbed in, finished the serial.

It was always a little disconcerting to watch Bela Lugosi doing serial duty. He had become so closely identified with the character of Dracula, his most famous role, that one was constantly waiting for the fanged teeth and accompanying bite-in-the-neck to appear. Instead, we found only routine treachery in titles like *The Whispering Shadow* and *SOS Coast Guard*. In *The Phantom Creeps* he utilized the services of one of the strangest-looking robots to ever grace the screen.

Robots were also on the mind of Eduardo Ciannelli as the *Mysterious Doctor Satan*. He wanted to build an army of them and rule the world, but he seemed to have his hands full with only one as The Copperhead, his masked pursuer, brought an end to his mad dreams. For some reason Republic requested that Ciannelli be billed as Edward rather than Eduardo. The script for *Mysterious Doctor Satan* was originally intended for an adventure featuring the Superman comic character, but when negotiations fell through it was revised for this more pedestrian tale.

It may seem to some inappropriate to label any performance in a serial as being classic, but such an accolade was richly deserved by Henry Brandon for his portrayal of the title character in *Drums of Fu Manchu*. With his high-pitched voice frequently cracking as his hysteria increased, Fu Manchu led his pursuers on a treacherous chase as he sought to obtain a sacred scepter that would give him power over the hillmen he needed to support him in his mad quest for power. The last chapter of *Drums of Fu Manchu*, unlike the majority of serials, found the chief malefactor quite alive and vowing to return to unleash his wrath once again.

One of the serials' hardest working actors was George J. Lewis. Though appearing from time to time as a hero in films like *The Wolf Dog* and *Zorro's Black Whip*, Lewis' forte was as an action heavy, engaging in fight after fight as he followed the orders of ruthless leaders in serials like *Captain America, G-Men vs. the Black Dragon, Daredevils of the West, Haunted Harbor* and *The Tiger Woman*. His favorite role was that of the dapper, piano-playing Jim Belmont in *Federal Operator 99*. Unlike many of his roles, this one offered him a chance to create a different kind of villain. Somehow an order to steal or kill seemed a bit more horrible coming from the lips of a man sitting behind a piano and playing the "Moonlight Sonata".

An equally gifted and often utilized performer was Roy Barcroft. For many years Republic's favorite bad guy in dozens of B-Westerns, Barcroft graced the casts of numerous serials like *Son of Zorro, King of the Texas Rangers,*

Left, Edward (changed from Eduardo for this serial) Ciannelli planned to conquer the world with an army of robots in *Mysterious Doctor Satan* (Republic, 1940).

Jesse James Rides Again, Daughter of Don Q and *Haunted Harbor.* His two best roles (and his own personal favorites) were as the title character in *The Purple Monster Strikes* and as Captain Mephisto in *Manhunt of Mystery Island.* In the former serial he was an alien from Mars who, after landing on Earth, had to build a spaceship to return to his own planet and went about it by using guns, cars, trucks, etc.; in the latter he was the reincarnation of a pirate after a newly-developed power machine.

Over at Columbia James Craven was always good for a few laughs as he seemed always to play a hypertensive villain in vehicles like *The Green Archer, White Eagle* and *Captain Midnight.* His henchmen never could do anything right, and Craven's ranting and raving grew progressively wilder with each chapter.

Trevor Bardette was more at home in feature productions, but his villainous masquerades in *Overland with Kit Carson* and *Jungle Girl* were noteworthy. In *Jungle Girl* he was cast in a dual role and murdered his twin brother in order to get a valuable cache of diamonds.

In a very real sense, the serials had their own stock company of players who were able to adapt themselves to virtually any situation. In one serial they might be the right-hand man of the lead villain while in another they might just do a brief sequence in a single chapter, receiving no billing whatsoever. Men like Anthony Warde, Kenne Duncan and Bud Geary were always involved, it seemed, in an endless parade of fisticuffs, car chases, bombings and shootings at the behest of their insatiable leaders. John Piccori seemed comfortable playing deformities like Gould in *Fighting Devil Dogs* and Moloch in *Dick Tracy.* Tristram Coffin and I. Stanford Jolley were equally adept at playing contemporary or B-Western tyrants, while other quality performers like Neil Hamilton, Noah Beery, Sr., Cy Kendall and others made their occasional forays into serial productions memorable.

Villainy was not the exclusive prerogative of men in the serials. Many excellent performances were turned in by the distaff side as well. Carol Forman was equally venomous playing Sombra in *The Black Widow* and The Spider Lady who tried to bring an end to The Man of Steel's career in *Superman.* Forman was less flamboyant but equally ruthless in *Federal Agents vs. Underworld, Inc.* trying to acquire a pair of golden hands that would unlock a valuable secret, and in *Blackhawk* where, as Laska, she was the head of a vicious sabotage ring.

Lorna Gray almost matched George J. Lewis in the dexterity with which she was able to shift between playing good roles and bad ones. In serials like *Captain America, Deadwood Dick* and *Flying G-Men* she gave quite acceptable support to the leading men and, after she changed her name to Adrian Booth, was able to stand quite capably on her own as the star of *Daughter of Don Q.* However, Gray's most famous role, and the one most appreciated by her fans, was that of the evil Vultura in *Perils of Nyoka.* Assisted by her bloodthirsty underlings and a fiercely loyal ape, Satan, Vultura was after the long lost "Tablets of Hippocrates," hoping to find on them the secret to a valuable treasure trove. It took stars Kay Aldridge and Clayton Moore fifteen well-scripted episodes to finally catch Vultura, but it was Satan who delivered the fatal spear thrust that ended her reign of terror. Such was her value at the box office at the time, having made a number of quality B-films, Gray was able to command a bigger salary for her role than Kay Aldridge was able to get as the star of *Perils of Nyoka.* Another memorable Lorna Gray role was that of Rita Parker in *Federal Operator 99.* As George J. Lewis' right-hand woman, Gray was more than handy with a gun until her own boss fired the fatal shots that ended her life.

Other important female contributions to the serial rogues' gallery included Priscilla Lawson as Ming's daughter, Aura, in *Flash Gordon,* Evelyn Brent as Shanghai Lil in *Jungle Jim,* Gloria Franklin as Fu Manchu's daughter, Fah Lo Suee, in *Drums of Fu Manchu* and Rose Hobart as Frauline Von Teufel in *Adventures of Smilin' Jack.*

To look quite objectively at the serials one has to admit that although the heroes received all the adulation and attention, the villains really provided the motivations and thrills that made the genre work effectively as an entertainment form. They were ruthless, power-crazed and murderous in the extreme, and we couldn't wait for Saturday to come so that we could delight in their machinations.

For most people, the most famous serial villain of all time was Charles Middleton as Ming the Merciless in the three Flash Gordon serials. This scene is from *Flash Gordon's Trip to Mars* (Universal, 1938).

In addition to playing Ming the Merciless, another favorite Charles Middleton role was the vengeance-seeking 39013 in *Daredevils of the Red Circle* (Republic, 1939).

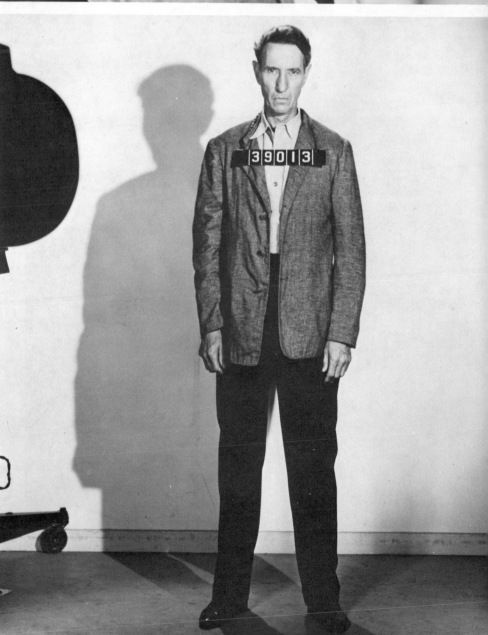

Top left, Mary Moore, at the time the wife of Clayton Moore, gave some short-lived help to her master in *The Purple Monster Strikes* (Republic, 1945).

Top right, Tristram Coffin in one of his early serial ventures as a bad guy, *Holt of the Secret Service* (Columbia, 1941).

Left, Anthony Warde was very likely Republic's most-used action heavy. Here singer Stuart Hamblem, in a rare film appearance, gives him some necessary information in *King of the Forest Rangers* (Republic, 1946).

Top right, Frequently utilized heavy Bud Geary keeps his gun on George Chesebro while Fred Graham convinces him he should do a little talking. When that didn't work, they tried acid in *The Purple Monster Strikes* (Republic, 1945).

Right, The evil duo who sought to sabotage our war effort during World War II was Johnny Arthur as Sakima, a radical departure from his usual comic roles, and William Forrest, who received top-billing in *The Masked Marvel* (Republic, 1943).

125

Left, George J. Lewis was the sophisticated, piano-playing villain of *Federal Operator 99* (Republic, 1945). His cohorts in crime were the oft-used LeRoy Mason and Hal Taliaferro (formerly B-Western star Wally Wales).

Bottom left, Neil Hamilton was a first-rate agent of deceit in *King of the Texas Rangers* (Republic, 1941).

Bottom right, One of the really big stars to appear as a serial villain was Charles Bickford in *Riders of Death Valley* (Universal, 1941). On the left is Roy Barcroft and on the right, Jack Rockwell.

Right, Roy Barcroft was at his malevolent best in *The Purple Monster Strikes* (Republic, 1945) as a visitor from Mars.

Right, After serving Roy Barcroft loyally for fifteen episodes Kenne Duncan is rewarded with a bullet in *Haunted Harbor* (Republic, 1944).

Left, Poor Noah Beery, Sr. received a similar reward from Harry Worth in *Adventures of Red Ryder* (Republic, 1940), but he only had to work for twelve chapters.

Left, Bela Lugosi wins our award for creating the silliest looking robot in serials for *The Phantom Creeps* (Universal, 1939).

Right, James Craven, seated, was Columbia's favorite "brains" heavy. He was a delight as he ranted and raved at his underlings in chapter after chapter, becoming more distraught as each week went by. Here, in *The Green Archer* (Columbia, 1940), he instructs a bogus Green Archer, Jack Ingram, to commit more mayhem while Robert Fiske, another Columbia mainstay, looks on.

129

Above, Cy Kendall was appropriately evil in *Secret Agent X-9* (Universal, 1945).

Right, Evelyn Brent was the notorious Shanghai Lil in *Jungle Jim* (Universal, 1937).

Below left, Trevor Bardette has finally located the diamonds he killed his twin brother to get in *Jungle Girl* (Republic, 1941).

Below right, John Piccori specialized in playing diabolical henchmen like Porotu in *Robinson Crusoe of Clipper Island* (Republic, 1936).

Far right, Lorna Gray's Vultura in *Perils of Nyoka* (Republic, 1942) was a memorable characterization and she got paid more for it than the serial's star, Kay Aldridge.

Above, One of the finest serial portrayals was that of Henry Brandon as Fu Manchu in *Drums of Fu Manchu* (Republic, 1940).

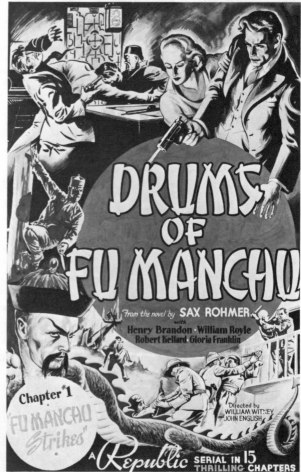

Right, Carol Forman as *The Black Widow* (Republic, 1947) was an excellent exercise in female aggressiveness as she murdered her victims remorselessly.

Below, A final trio of malcontents: Lionel Atwill as The Scarab with his henchmen John Davidson and George J. Lewis in *Captain America* (Republic, 1944).

10 LADIES TO THE RESCUE

THE EXCITING, COLORFUL days of serial queens like Pearl White, Ruth Roland and Helen Holmes in silent films gave way to the realities of male chauvinism when sound came in. The very nature of the serial, with its accent on fights, chases and strenuous physical action, generally precluded women from playing a dominant role. Although every serial had a female co-star, it was her duty primarily to be placed in peril, from which she was heroically rescued by the leading man, or she was consistently knocked unconscious in order to allow a fight sequence to proceed uncomplicated by her presence.

The early thirties saw only four women who appeared often enough in serials to qualify as effective heroines: Louise Lorraine in *The Lightning Express* and *The Jade Box;* Cecelia Parker in *The Jungle Mystery, The Lost Special* and *The Lost Jungle;* Dorothy Gulliver in *The Galloping Ghost, The Phantom of the West, The Last Frontier* and *The Shadow of the Eagle;* and Lucile Browne in *Battling With Buffalo Bill, The Airmail Mystery* (in which she co-starred with her husband, James Flavin), *Danger Island, The Law of the Wild* and *Mystery Squadron.*

Universal vainly tried to recapture the flavor of the serial heroine in 1934 with Evalyn Knapp starring in *Perils of Pauline.* It was a routine affair about the search for the formula of a deadly gas, and hero Robert Allen had most of the important footage. Universal did succeed in promoting one charming woman into serial star status in the thirties in the person of blonde Jean Rogers. In adventures like *Tailspin Tommy in the Great Air Mystery, Secret Agent X-9, Ace Drummond* and *The Adventures of Frank Merriwell* she was a decided asset to her leading men, but it was as Dale Arden in *Flash Gordon* and *Flash Gordon's Trip to Mars* that she achieved serial immortality. Constantly being leered at and lusted after by Ming the Merciless, Dale Arden managed to scream and faint with alarming regularity until Flash came to the rescue.

Columbia had a difficult enough time trying to create suitable scripts for their leading men without trying to create something for their heroes' female companions. Lovely Iris Meredith was very likely the studio's most effective co-star, appearing in *Overland With Kit Carson,*

The Spider's Web and *The Green Archer,* as well as being featured in many B-Westerns. Dorothy Fay (Tex Ritter's wife) also made a lot of B-Westerns and wound up in serials like *White Eagle* and *The Green Archer.* Columbia was famous for churning out interesting little B-films and many of the female stars of these little gems would take a fling at serial work: Joan Woodbury as *Brenda Starr, Reporter;* Veda Ann Borg as Margot Lane in *The Shadow* and as Cora in *Jungle Raiders;* Evelyn Brent in *Holt of the Secret Service;* Adele Jergens in *Black Arrow;* Jennifer Holt in *Hop Harrigan;* and Noel Neill in *Superman* and *Atom Man vs. Superman.* There were many others, of course: beauty contest winners, starlets trying to make a name, old stars taking one last fling—all of whom quietly deserted the motion picture screen for the security of marriage and other less volatile careers.

It was left to Republic to restore women to a place of prominence in the serial field, and they did a first-rate job. In 1941 the studio acquired rights to Edgar Rice Burrough's *Jungle Girl.* Using the book's title (but nothing else) they fashioned an exciting fifteen-chapter adventure in which beautiful Frances Gifford was cast as Nyoka. Wearing a fetching costume, Gifford gave an extremely effective performance in a tale which found her trying to prevent the theft of valuable diamonds. Leaping from cliffs, swinging through the jungle on vines, fighting lions (though everything was accomplished with the aid of stuntmen), Gifford gave young audiences an opportunity to see an active heroine at work. *Jungle Girl* was a critical and commercial success and Republic scheduled a sequel, *Perils of Nyoka,* for production the following year, also to star Gifford. However, due to various legal tangles involving character rights with the copyright holders, when *Perils of Nyoka* reached the screen it was with Kay Aldridge starring as Nyoka.

It was a lucky break for Aldridge who, up to this point, had only made a few minor appearances in features. She was to become Republic's first advertised serial queen, appearing in three of their very best serials: *Perils of Nyoka, Daredevils of the West* and *Haunted Harbor.* In *Perils of Nyoka* she co-starred with Clayton Moore, who would go on to achieve lasting fame as television's Lone

Kay Aldridge was Republic's first serial queen of the forties. She appears here in a portrait from *Daredevils of the West* (Republic, 1943), one of the most action-packed serials ever made.

Ranger in the fifties, in an adventure which found her trapped in spike-laden pits, threatened by a pendulum-like blade, and almost blown off the side of a cliff by cyclonic-force winds in a tunnel—all of which made Nyoka's perils colorful, to say the least. In *Daredevils of the West,* the most action-packed of all Republic's Western serial adventures, Aldridge had the assistance of Allan Lane in helping prevent a ruthless gang of marauders from stopping the development of her stagecoach line. Some of the fight sequences staged for *Daredevils of the West* remain unequalled for their choreographed inventiveness. Aldridge's final serial appearance was in *Haunted Harbor,* a sea and island thriller that found her helping Kane Richmond clear himself of a framed murder charge. Kay seemed to be knocked unconscious more than was required of the average serial heroine in this fifteen-chapter tale, but it was all appealing to matinee fans.

When Aldridge left Republic in 1944 it looked as though there might not be a successor to the "Queen of the Serials." Fortunately, such was not to be the case. Linda Stirling, a tall, willowy fashion model was standing in the wings, waiting to become the sound serial's most popular heroine. Stirling's debut as *The Tiger Woman,* with Allan Lane giving physical support, was an imaginative introduction that found her ruling a tribe whose land contained vast oil deposits. She was at her engaging best sentencing evildoers to a fiery death in the volcanic pits beneath her temple and engaging villain George J. Lewis in acrobatic fight sequences. After *The Tiger Woman,* Stirling put on another costume to essay the role of The Whip in the Western thriller, *Zorro's Black Whip.* There was a lot of riding and whip-cracking, but most of the rugged action was left to hero George J. Lewis, playing a sympathetic role in a change of pace from his usual heavy roles. In *Manhunt of Mystery Island* she and co-star Richard Bailey travelled to Mystery Island in search of her kidnapped father and his "Radiatomic Power Transmitter." Opposing them was Roy Barcroft as the mysterious Captain Mephisto, and for fifteen episodes we watched Linda nearly being drowned, blown-up or otherwise imperiled until, in the final reel, it was she who delivered the final bullet that ended Mephisto's "piratical swashbuckling." As if battling reincarnated pirates wasn't enough, that same year she had to contend with Roy Barcroft once again, only this time he

was an emissary from the planet Mars in *The Purple Monster Strikes.* Her perils were even greater this time around as she was almost killed in a rocket blast, drowned in a water-filling pit and facing what seemed certain death in a plunge off a cliff. Things began to get a little less hectic in her fifth adventure, *The Crimson Ghost.* In this fanciful tale she and Charles Quigley were after a mysterious madman out to build a large-scale model of a death-dealing device called a "Cyclotrode." After a mere twelve chapters the chase was at an end, The Crimson Ghost unmasked, and Linda was heading for the Western setting of her final serial, *Jesse James Rides Again.* Linda had apparently come full circle, for this time around, as in *The Tiger Woman,* the villains were once again after hidden oil deposits. Coming to her frequent rescue was Clayton Moore, glorifying the role of badman Jesse James. After this serial Linda had decided enough was enough, and she retreated to the relative quiet of married life, becoming Mrs. Sloan Nibley (Nibley was to write many screenplays for Republic's Roy Rogers series).

The only woman at Republic who might have challenged Linda Stirling's serial tenure was Peggy Stewart, but she was kept so busy doing the studio's B-Westerns that she only had time to make two serials, *Son of Zorro* and *The Phantom Rider.* (Over at Columbia she also made *Tex Granger* and *Cody of the Pony Express.)* Peggy, an excellent rider, was always strong-willed and forceful in her Western portrayals, unlike so many heroines who looked continually helpless and weak. Along with Buster Crabbe, Kirk Alyn and Noel Neill, Stewart is a much-sought-after guest at the various nostalgia conventions which take place each year.

Republic also had some important female portrayals by Louise Currie in *Adventures of Captain Marvel* and *The Masked Marvel,* Helen Talbot in *Federal Operator 99* and *King of the Forest Rangers,* Marguerite Chapman in *Spy Smasher* and Adrian Booth as the *Daughter of Don Q.* As Republic headed down the stretch toward serial oblivion, with decreasing budgets and waning quality, it fell to Aline Towne, Phyllis Coates, Noel Neill, Ramsay Ames, Rosemary LaPlanche and Pamela Blake to do the best they could to keep things moving in a lively fashion. Clearly the days of the serial queen had ended, and the demise of the serial itself would soon follow.

Right, Adrian Booth (formerly Lorna Gray) and Kirk Alyn obtain an important painting from Dale Van Sickel. Director Spencer Gordon Bennet posed for the oil which held a valuable secret printed on the scroll, in *Daughter of Don Q* (Republic, 1946).

Below, Ted Mapes is about to show Carole Mathews the intricacies of a death-dealing furnace in *The Monster and the Ape* (Columbia, 1945).

Above, Joan Marsh shows that she's no pushover in *Secret Service in Darkest Africa* (Republic, 1943).

Left, Peggy Stewart was a favorite B-Western heroine and carried her acting talents into serials like *Tex Granger* (Columbia, 1948).

Top left, as *The Tiger Woman* (Republic, 1944) Linda Stirling started many a serial fan's heart beating a little faster.

Top right, Columbia's favorite leading lady was beautiful Iris Meredith, here in a publicity still for *The Spider's Web* (Columbia, 1938).

Left, Visiting director Frank Borzage shows veteran serial director Spencer Gordon Bennet how Helen Talbot's hands should be tied in this publicity shot for *King of the Forest Rangers* (Republic, 1946).

Right, Although she made other serials, Noel Neill will always be remembered as Lois Lane in *Superman* (Columbia, 1948).

Below, Pretending to be a tough girl meant committing the ultimate sin—smoking a cigarette. Evelyn Brent pulled off the trick in *Holt of the Secret Service* (Columbia, 1941).

Below right, Louise Currie appealed to fans in *Adventures of Captain Marvel* and in this scene from *The Masked Marvel* (Republic, 1943).

Above, Each serial generally had one master set in which action would take place in various episodes. This is an extensive look at the master set for *The Tiger Woman* (Republic, 1944). Linda Stirling is on the throne and Allan Lane stands between the guards at the right.

DAUGHTER of DON Q

featuring

ADRIAN BOOTH
KIRK ALYN
LeROY MASON
ROY BARCROFT

A *Republic* SERIAL IN **12** CHAPTERS

DIRECTED BY
SPENCER BENNET and FRED BRANNON
ORIGINAL SCREEN PLAY BY
ALBERT DeMOND — BASIL DICKEY — JESSE DUFFY
LYNN PERKINS

Chapter **1.** MULTIPLE MURDER

Right, One of the deadly perils Kay Aldridge and Forbes Murray faced were these spikes in *Perils of Nyoka* (Republic, 1942).

Below Lorna Gray bounced around in serials as both heroine and villainess. In *Flying G-Men* (Columbia, 1939) she was a good girl.

Below right, Marguerite Chapman was one of the few serial heroines who went on to major features. Here she consoles a dying Kane Richmond in *Spy Smasher* (Republic, 1942).

11 GUARDIANS OF THE GLOBE

CRITICS MAY FAULT the serials for many things, but a lack of variety is certainly not one of them. The creative imaginations of writers like Basil Dickey, Joseph Poland, Barney Sarecky, George H. Plympton, and Ronald Davidson (among many others) were given free rein to craft screenplays that pictured a world beset by malcontents not only of the present, but the past and future as well.

Columbia ventured from the more traditional serial plots to give audiences a taste of earlier historical periods in several films of the forties and fifties. In *The Desert Hawk* dashing Gilbert Roland played a dual role as a recently-crowned caliph and a villainous brother who sought to take over the throne. Roland cut a dashing figure riding over the desert sands wearing his coat of mail with the figure of a hawk emblazoned upon the chest, meting out justice to villains. *Son of the Guardsman* was set in the days of Robin Hood, with star Robert Shaw combating robber barons and wicked regents with equal skill and derring-do. One of the studio's better efforts was put forward in *Adventures of Sir Galahad* with George Reeves (later to gain fame as television's Superman) portraying the famous legendary knight who had to find the sword Excalibur in order to gain admittance to King Arthur's famed Round Table. Along the perilous path to success lay a villainous magician, a mysterious outlaw known as The Black Knight and sundry murderous Saxon bandits. Part of the fun of watching this serial was in seeing veteran Western heavy Charles King play a comic foil—a type of role he began his career with in silent films. King engaged in various slapstick sequences, even donning a dress when the situation called for such an extreme. Swashbuckling was the order of the day in *The Great Adventures of Captain Kidd* as hero Richard Crane allied himself with the famous pirate in order to combat a ruthless band of cutthroats who were pillaging and looting while Kidd received the undeserved blame. All of these serial adventures made extensive use of stock footage from Columbia's earlier costume film productions.

On a more current level, law-enforcement officials of almost every type found their sagas against crime being presented in serial formats. The most-represented of this gallant legion were our friends in Canada, the Royal Canadian Mounted Police. All three of the major serial-producing companies filmed Mountie tales which, for obvious commercial advantage, were nothing more than glorified Westerns done in more picturesque surroundings. Universal's contributions were *Clancy of the Mounted* (1933), in which Tom Tyler stalked a gang who had framed his brother for murder, and *The Royal Mounted Rides Again* (1945), with Bill Kennedy starring in an incredibly dull story about outlaws after a fortune in gold. Columbia ventured into the North Country for four of its thrillers. In *The Mysterious Pilot,* the celebrated real-life air ace, Captain Frank Hawks, played the protector of a young girl (Dorothy Sebastian) menaced by a ruthless killer who feared she would unmask his villainy. At the end of each chapter of *The Mysterious Pilot* Hawks would conduct a small demonstration on some aerial topic to an attentive young boy. The only other time this gimmick was used was in *The Secret Code* when audiences were treated to lessons in how to break enemy codes. In *Perils of the Royal Mounted* Robert Stevens (who also was billed in serials as Robert Kellard) was a Mountie sergeant after a vicious gang that was inciting the Indians to go on the warpath. *Gunfighters of the Northwest* gave stuntman-actor Jock Mahoney ample opportunity to demonstrate his considerable abilities in a tale that was filmed completely outdoors without the use of a single interior set, something extremely rare in movie production. Even a scene supposedly set in a cave was staged by director Spencer Bennet in such a way that shadows gave the impression you were inside when you really were not. Columbia's last Canadian serial was a tepid, stock-laden affair called *Perils of the Wilderness* in which Dennis Moore and Richard Emory pitted themselves against murderous Indian agitators and gunrunners.

Republic also turned Northward for four serial escapades. In *King of the Royal Mounted,* Allan Lane played a Mountie sergeant who captured a gang of spies after a secret mixture called "Compound X" that could render enemy mines ineffective. In *King of the Mounties,* Lane dealt a death blow to the Axis Fifth Column in Canada who were terrorizing the populace with bombing raids from a mysterious plane called The Falcon. These two

Allan Lane serials firmly established the actor as a leading Republic hero, and are among the most thrilling productions (with beautifully staged fight sequences and wonderful miniature work) ever made for Saturday matinee fans. *Dangers of the Canadian Mounted* (1948) presented Jim Bannon, a veteran radio and film actor, as a Mountie Captain after a mysterious "Chief" who was leading a gang in search of "liquid" diamonds. Republic bade farewell to Canada with *Canadian Mounties vs. Atomic Invaders* in 1953 with Bill Henry trying to stop Arthur Space and his cohorts from building a series of rocket-launching platforms from which they intended to fire missiles against the United States.

Meanwhile, back in this country, our own agents were busily at work. In *King of the Forest Rangers* Larry Thompson had his hands full trying to stop Stuart Hamblen from gaining a mineral treasure located under the sites of some old Indian towers. Robert Paige was the masked hero of *Flying G-Men*, called The Black Falcon who sought to thwart the plans of enemy agents to acquire a new type of plane. In *Flying G-Men* youngster Sammy McKim was the head of a group called the Junior Air Defenders who also assisted The Black Falcon. This was a gimmick the studio used strictly for commercial purposes making membership (including an "official" badge) available to youngsters who came to see all fifteen chapters of the serial. Audience identification with young players in various serials proved effective in the thirties, but the practice was generally given up in the forties when scriptwriters found that the inclusion of these children tended to slow down the plot and make action sequences unnecessarily complicated. Obviously, a hero couldn't do his best work if he was always watching out for a young ward.

Youth did have a fling in adventures such as *Junior G-Men*, *Junior G-Men of the Air* and *Sea Raiders* which featured The East Side Kids (a group which changed as different members were added or deleted from the clan). Even that most revered of all groups, the Boy Scouts of America, was represented by two films: the amateurish *Young Eagles* and the much-better *Scouts to the Rescue* with Jackie Cooper leading his scout pack in capturing a bunch of counterfeiters. *Scouts to the Rescue* used a trick

of having an Indian tribe speak a strange language which in reality was nothing more than a reversed soundtrack, something that would also be done in *Flash Gordon Conquers the Universe* for The Rock Men.

Armed forces agents as well as secret agents were featured in *SOS Coast Guard*, with Ralph Byrd tracking down Bela Lugosi and his deadly gas bombs; *Robinson Crusoe of Clipper Island*, with native actor Ray Mala playing a government operative in pursuit of a spy and sabotage ring headed by a mystery man known only as "H. K."; *Holt of the Secret Service*, with Jack Holt playing himself on the trail of a ring of counterfeiters; *Fighting Devil Dogs*, one of Republic's all-time favorite tales, in which Lee Powell and Herman Brix were two Marines after a deadly enemy called The Lightning; and a less-distinguished string of routine outings like *Government Agents vs. Phantom Legion*, *G-Men Never Forget*, *Federal Agents vs. Underworld, Inc.* and *Radar Patrol vs. Spy King*, to name just a few.

With the past and present seemingly well taken care of, our serial heroes eventually turned to enemies from outer space. In *Radar Men from the Moon*, George Wallace introduced a new character called Commando Cody, Sky Marshal of the Universe, who battled a villainous Roy Barcroft (wearing the same basic make-up he had used in an earlier science-fiction adventure, *The Purple Monster Strikes*, to match stock footage) bent on taking over the Earth from his headquarters on the Moon. *Zombies of the Stratosphere*, starred Judd Holdren, who prevented aliens from another world from setting off an atomic bomb that would throw Earth from its normal orbit around the sun. *Flying Disc Man from Mars* found Walter Reed trying desperately to prevent a menace from Mars from developing a new fleet of atomic-powered planes which could be used to dominate the Earth. Even a science-fiction classic from Jules Verne was given serial life when Columbia brought his *Mysterious Island* (albeit very freely adapted) to the screen in 1951 with Richard Crane as a hero trying to prevent a ruthless madman from creating a death-dealing explosive that could destroy the world.

With excellent guardians of freedom like these at work, America (or at least Saturday audiences) could rest easy.

Right, Columbia Pictures' head, Harry Cohn, forced star Jack Holt to do serial duty in *Holt of the Secret Service* (Columbia, 1941).

Below, Frank Coghlan, Jr., Vondell Darr and Jackie Cooper do some sleuthing in *Scouts to the Rescue* (Universal, 1939).

Above, Self-sacrifice was an important ingredient of serials. Robert Kellard sacrificed himself to save Allan Lane by sending him out through the torpedo tube when the compartment flooded in *King of the Royal Mounted* (Republic, 1940).

Left, George Wallace donned a rocket suit to portray Commando Cody in *Radar Men from the Moon* (Republic, 1952). This serial spawned a television series of twelve episodes, each complete in itself, that were also released to theaters.

Above right, In *Robinson Crusoe of Clipper Island* (Republic, 1936) Mala faces certain death in a fiery pit at the end of Chapter Two.

Right, Ralph Byrd has a tough task ahead when he tries to best huge Richard Alexander in *SOS Coast Guard* (Republic, 1937).

148

Right, Robert Shaw and Robert "Buzz" Henry swashbuckled their way through the awful *Son of the Guardsman* (Columbia, 1946).

Below, At the end of each chapter of *The Mysterious Pilot* (Columbia, 1937) air ace Frank Hawks gave audiences a flight lesson.

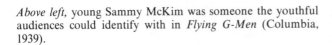

Above left, young Sammy McKim was someone the youthful audiences could identify with in *Flying G-Men* (Columbia, 1939).

Above right, Tristram Coffin, after years of playing villains, became the *King of the Rocket Men* (Republic, 1949).

Right, leaping from the pages of Jules Verne's *Mysterious Island* (Columbia, 1951) was Richard Crane as Captain Harding.

Top left, Kirk Alyn gets the drop on heavies Eddie Parker, John Crawford and Anthony Warde in *Radar Patrol vs. Spy King* (Republic, 1950). This sequence utilized stock from the earlier *G-Men vs. The Black Dragon.*

Bottom left, Jim Bannon protects himself against an attack by Ken Terrell in *Dangers of the Canadian Mounted* (Republic, 1948).

Right, Robert Lowery meets half of *The Monster and the Ape* (Columbia, 1945) in a better-than-average Columbia offering.

Below, in *Zombies of the Stratosphere* (Republic, 1952) Aline Towne, Judd Holdren and Wilson Wood confront the familiar robot from the earlier *Mysterious Doctor Satan.*

Top left, Robert Paige was the masked hero of *Flying G-Men* (Columbia, 1939) known as The Black Falcon.

Bottom left, George Reeves and Charles King seemed like an unlikely duo to match wits and swords with villains in *Adventures of Sir Galahad* (Columbia, 1949).

Right, Herman Brix and Lee Powell were the *Fighting Devil Dogs* (Republic, 1938) who finally uncovered The Lightning.

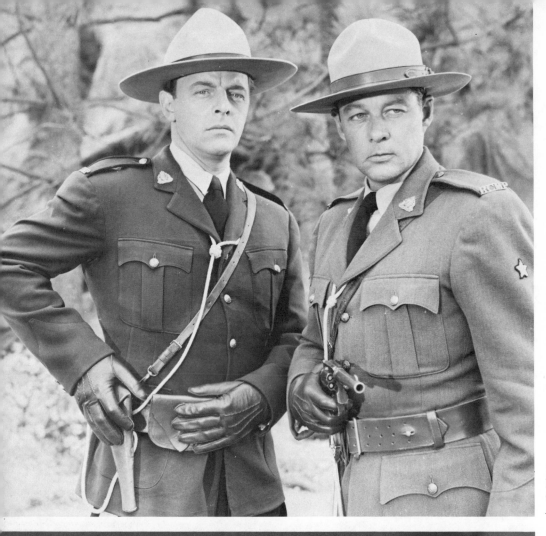

Top left, Harry Lauter and Bill Henry did their best for the honor of Canada in *Canadian Mounties vs. Atomic Invaders* (Republic, 1953).

Bottom left, The Desert Hawk (Columbia, 1944) featured the swordplay and horseplay of Gilbert Roland and Mona Maris.

Above, Robert Kellard gets his man in *Perils of the Royal Mounted* (Columbia, 1942).

Above right, Larry Thompson rescues Helen Talbot from a forest fire in *King of the Forest Rangers* (Republic, 1946).

Right, Richard Webb and Aline Towne fought against The Phantom Ruler in *The Invisible Monster* (Republic, 1950).

DURING THE GREAT DAYS of the silent serial it was a highly-publicized fact that many stars like Pearl White, Ruth Roland, Helen Holmes, Walter Miller and Joe Bonomo did their own incredible screen stunts. This individualistic excursion into heroics, however, was limited to a small group of serial players, while the majority were forced to adhere to studio production reality. A serial producer simply could not afford to let an injury to his star force an entire company to suspend shooting. Expediency, therefore, brought forth the formation of a small group of dedicated men and women who were willing to risk their lives for little pay and no screen credit: the stuntmen.

The twenties spawned a particularly noteworthy number of these illustrious daredevils, the most famous of whom was Yakima Canutt. An accomplished horseman and rodeo star, Canutt specialized in trick riding, roping, horse falls and similar stunts, and doubled in the action sequences for most of the era's Western and serial stars. In the thirties Canutt found himself playing on-screen roles as a villain in scores of features ranging from low-grade B-Westerns and serials to major epics like *Gone With the Wind.* As the years passed he became a top second-unit director, staging such memorable scenes as the chariot race in *Ben-Hur* and the battle scenes for *Khartoum.* In 1966 Canutt was given a special Academy Award for his achievements as a stuntman for developing safety devices to protect his fellow craftsmen. Canutt taught many stars to ride well and to stage fight sequences convincingly on the screen, but he takes particular pride in having helped make one of them, John Wayne, a screen immortal.

Following close on the heels of Canutt was another excellent horseman, Cliff Lyons, who did stunt work for stars like Buck Jones and Ken Maynard. Lyons, heavy-set and ruggedly built, like Canutt found himself playing roles as villains (as well as an occasional good guy) as the years progressed until he, too, became a second-unit director of merit.

Many stuntmen had a particular specialty in the field, and were always called upon when a particular thrill demanded their expertise: Al Wilson for daredevil aerial feats, Charles Hutchinson for motorcycle work, Helen

Gibson for every conceivable type of train work, and Leo Noomis for spectacular car crashes.

As the serial entered its third decade of production, a new and versatile group of daredevils entered the expanding field. David Sharpe began his screen career working on the Hal Roach lot doing two-reel comedies in which his athletic experience as a gymnast was fully tested doing an incredible array of acrobatic stunts. His work in the thirties alternated between playing minor on-screen roles and doing stunt work. One of the great serial anachronisms is to find David Sharpe, acknowledged as one of the best stuntmen in the business, starring as one of the leads in *Daredevils of the Red Circle* and being doubled in many sequences by young Jimmy Fawcett. Sharpe's best-remembered serial work was at Republic in the early forties before he went into service during World War II. In *Adventures of Red Ryder* (doubling for Don "Red" Barry), *Drums of Fu Manchu* (doubling for Robert Kellard), *Mysterious Doctor Satan* (doubling for Robert Wilcox), *Jungle Girl* (doubling for Tom Neal *and* Frances Gifford) and other outstanding films, Sharpe's creative staging of fights, leaps and chases remain unequalled highlights of the period. In *Adventures of Captain Marvel,* Sharpe's intercut footage for star Tom Tyler almost convinced the audience that Marvel really could fly as the young stunt ace leaped from cliffs, over cars, etc. Today, over sixty-five years of age and looking back upon a brilliant career as a solo performer and second-unit director, Sharpe is still hard at work in his field—and, when the mood strikes him, he will gladly do a complete back flip for an appreciative fan.

Probably no one worked harder as a stuntman in the serials than Tom Steele. Steele began his career as an actor in the early thirties, but gave up that end of the business to become a seasoned stuntman performing hazardous work for all four serial-producing companies. His work at Mascot, Universal and Columbia could be described as routine in comparison to the incredible amount of work he put in at Republic, where he was the head of the studio's stunt team for most of the forties through the demise of serial production in the fifties. During those hard-working

Left, Richard Talmadge, one of the greatest stuntmen of all time, in *Pirate Treasure* (Universal, 1934). Despite his presence, this serial had only a few stunts and was terribly disappointing to Talmadge fans who expected nothing but action.

years Steele doubled for almost every serial lead or lead heavy, as well as for many of the studio's B-Western stars such as William Elliott, Allan Lane and Sunset Carson. Tall, slim and versatile, Steele was equally adept at horse work, falls, and leaps. As was the case with most of the stunt stars, in any given serial you could count on Steele to appear in bit roles in several chapters, usually getting killed off in a gun fight. This was fine when fans only saw one chapter a week and had no way of checking back on an earlier episode, but it became very disconcerting when the serials were later edited into features and you kept seeing the same man getting killed and reappearing every few minutes. Steele probably had his best role as the title character in *The Masked Marvel,* in which he not only played the lead (without receiving any screen credit at all) but doubled in the fight sequences for the four actors suspected of being The Marvel, as well as making an appearance as a quickly-dispatched villain. Steele is still trim and fit and has continued his career of action work, particularly at the Walt Disney studios.

Steele's frequent companion in serial mayhem at Republic was Dale Van Sickel, who doubled for the more heavy-set leads (like Charles Quigley and Kirk Alyn). Although Van Sickel's speciality was car and motorcycle work (he did many of the spectacular sequences in *On the Beach* and the more recent *Duel),* the serial aficionado looks back with fondness upon the set-destroying fight sequences he and Steele did in films like *G-Men vs. the Black Dragon, Secret Service in Darkest Africa* and *The Masked Marvel.*

Although Sharpe, Steele and Van Sickel received most of the public's attention, they were supported by a talented group of supporting action stars: Fred Graham, who frequently doubled for master-villain Roy Barcroft; Eddie Parker, who doubled Buster Crabbe in his Universal serials and made frequent appearances for Republic; Ken Terrell who, like Sharpe, specialized in acrobatic fight sequences; Duke Green, who seemed to leap all over a set with apparent unconcern; George DeNormand, equally at ease doubling for a serial lead or a giant like Spencer Tracy; Carey Loftin, another automotive specialist (he drove the truck in *Duel);* Ted Mapes, able to shift from the Western domain of *Zorro's Fighting Legion* to an island adventure in *Hawk of the Wilderness.* There were, of course, many others—Harvey Parry, Johnny Dahiem, Joe and Bill Yrigoyen, and Jimmy Fawcett all deserve mention.

The easiest way to get a stuntman upset is to slight the female members of their profession. To a man they acknowledge that the ladies can more than hold their own in this dangerous fraternity of daredevils. I am therefore happy to express serial fans' deep appreciation to Helen Thurston (for work in *Jungle Girl* and *Perils of Nyoka),* Babe DeFreest (for serial adventures that included *Daredevils of the West* and *The Tiger Woman)* and Polly Burson (for *The Crimson Ghost* and *Son of Zorro)* as three outstanding members of the distaff contingent of action stars.

It would seem only natural that the best type of serial would be one in which a stuntman was the star. The two best examples of how this type of reasoning proved faulty were in *Pirate Treasure* and *Cody of the Pony Express.* In *Pirate Treasure* Richard Talmadge, one of the greatest action stars, merely had a few good stunts in the early chapters and then did virtually nothing for the remaining ten. Jock Mahoney in *Cody of the Pony Express* (who doubled for such heavyweights as Errol Flynn and Randolph Scott) did very little action work for the entire fifteen chapters (although he did fare a bit better in *Roar of the Iron Horse* and *Gunfighters of the Northwest).*

Although many people have the impression that stuntmen are a brawny and uneducated lot, quite the opposite is true. David Sharpe, Tom Steele, Dale Van Sickel (among others) are college-educated professionals who entered their screen careers with proven ability to dissect every stunt and determine its mathematical and physical requirements for margins of safety. Because of this training these men, who each have been in the business for more than forty years, have managed to survive with merely a collection of bumps and bruises—no serious injuries. From the riskiest tasks (boat-to-boat transfers in which spraying water made surfaces slippery and runaway wagons which were hard to guide) to everyday horse falls (that gave every stuntman a continuing series of sore spots), these men provided the thrills and excitement that made the serials the wonderful escapist entertainment we so fondly recall.

Dale Van Sickel, doubling for Dick Purcell, gives Ken Terrell a quick flip in *Captain America* (Republic, 1944).

David Sharpe, doubling for Kay Aldridge, makes a spectacular leap in *Perils of Nyoka* (Republic, 1942).

KING OF THE TEXAS RANGERS

A REPUBLIC SERIAL IN 12 CHAPTERS

Chapter 3 **MAN HUNT**

Left, David Sharpe, doubling for "Slingin' Sammy" Baugh, does his specialty for *King of the Texas Rangers* (Republic, 1941).

Below, David Sharpe, doubling for Kane Richmond, in an exciting fight sequence for *Spy Smasher* (Republic, 1942).

Right, David Sharpe doubling for Don "Red" Barry in a leap from *Adventures of Red Ryder* (Republic, 1940).

Left, Duke Green and a masked Tom Steele begin a typical Republic slugfest in *The Masked Marvel* (Republic, 1943).

Below, The success of *Adventures of Captain Marvel* (Republic, 1941) was due in no small degree to David Sharpe's doubling of star Tom Tyler in the action sequences.

Right, Helen Thurston, one of the best stuntwomen in the business, doubled for Frances Gifford in *Jungle Girl* (Republic, 1941).

Left, Jimmy Fawcett does a backflip while Ken Terrell attacks David Sharpe, doubling for Allan Lane, in *King of the Royal Mounted* (Republic, 1940).

Below, Dale Van Sickel, doubling for Dick Purcell, delivers one to the chin of fellow stunt ace Fred Graham in *Captain America* (Republic, 1944).

Right, Arms await to catch David Sharpe, doubling for Tristram Coffin, in *King of the Rocket Men* (Republic, 1949).

This sequence of four scenes from *Federal Agents vs. Underworld, Inc.* (Republic, 1949) shows how the studio utilized a single stuntman in succeeding chapters, assuming the audience had no way to remember how he might have been killed in an earlier episode. The first scene *(top left)* is from Chapter One and shows stuntman Tom Steele as Roy Barcroft's henchman. Scene two *(bottom left)* shows Steele as a pilot in Chapter Four. With the addition of a scar and mustache *(top right)*, Steele strikes again in Chapter Eight. Finally *(bottom right)*, in Chapter Twelve, with a new mustache and the assistance of Art Dillard, Steele makes his final nondoubling appearance.

Above, David Sharpe, doubling for Kay Aldridge, dives through an inferno in *Perils of Nyoka* (Republic, 1942).

Right, Eddie Parker, doubling for Grant Withers, is about to go over the falls in *Jungle Jim* (Universal, 1937).

172

Top left, Dale Van Sickel takes a wild ride doubling for Marten Lamont in *Federal Operator 99* (Republic, 1945).

Bottom left, Yakima Canutt.

Bottom right, A spectacular horse stunt by Canutt.

Right, Tom Steele does a convincing leap as Rod Cameron's double in *Secret Service in Darkest Africa* (Republic, 1943).

Below, David Sharpe does a slide-for-life doubling for "Slingin' Sammy" Baugh in *King of the Texas Rangers* (Republic, 1941).

Richard Bailey delivers a convincing punch to Dale Van Sickel, doubling for Roy Barcroft, in *Manhunt of Mystery Island* (Republic, 1945) and reveals why their hats never came off. Notice the rubber band holding Van Sickel's headgear in place.

Babe Defreest, another top-notch stuntwoman, doubled for Linda Stirling in *Zorro's Black Whip* (Republic, 1944).

ALTHOUGH SERIALS HAD an immensely devoted following, by far the most powerful lure to attract young fans into Saturday matinee screenings was the continuing parade of B-Western adventures featuring many of the screen's most popular idols of the day. Each year audiences flocked to see anywhere from six to eight new saddle tales featuring Buck Jones, Tim McCoy, Bob Steele, William Elliott (among others) and the producing companies quickly realized it would be to their advantage to feature these mounted heroes in a serial format where viewers could watch them for up to fifteen consecutive weeks. Western serials were always considered budget-savers by the studios; each had its own Western streets on the backlots or were close to nearby ranch locations, thereby saving money and shooting time.

Buck Jones was very likely the sound serial's most popular outdoor star, appearing in six productions. In *Gordon of Ghost City* (1933) Buck was after a gang of cattle rustlers who also had designs on a rich vein of gold. The following year in *The Red Rider* he risked his life repeatedly to save a friend (Grant Withers) from a framed murder charge. Riding his famous horse Silver, Buck saved a valuable mineral mine from a band of outlaw usurpers in *The Roaring West*. Hidden behind a white mask, he became *The Phantom Rider* to save a ranch from being stolen because a railroad planned to build through it, making it extremely valuable. In 1941 Buck made his fifth and final serial for Universal, the star-laden *Riders of Death Valley.* Surrounded by a cast including Dick Foran, Leo Carrillo, Charles Bickford, and Guinn "Big Boy" Williams, Buck was a member of a vigilante group trying to break up a protection racket bent on acquiring certain mining claims. The advertising claims that *Riders of Death Valley* was a "Million Dollar Serial" referred more to the value of the players than actual production costs for this otherwise routine Western adventure. Buck made one serial at Columbia, *White Eagle,* in which director James Horne had him engage in more than a few silly sequences. In 1942 the screen's dashing hero became one in real life when he sacrificed his life to save others in the tragic Boston Coconut Grove fire.

Johnny Mack Brown started his long film career

playing sophisticated leading men at MGM, but a rumored flirtation with Marion Davies, then the exclusive property of William Randolph Hearst, found him expelled from the lot. Johnny then went into Westerns and became one of the really top-flight cowboy stars. His first serial was Mascot's *Fighting with Kit Carson* in 1933. Johnny was the famous scout who was engaged in a fictional chase after a band of renegades called The Mystery Riders who were trying to locate a lost shipment of government gold. From Mascot Johnny moved to Universal where he appeared in *Rustlers of Red Dog* (protecting settlers from Indians and gold from robbers), *Wild West Days* (saving a mine from Indians and white men alike), *Flaming Frontiers* (saving another mine from more Indians and more evil white men), and finally, in 1939, *The Oregon Trail* (battling Indians and white men to save a wagon train). His serial work then behind him, Johnny Mack Brown concentrated solely on a long string of very successful Universal and Monogram B-Western features.

William "Wild Bill" Elliott also started out portraying tuxedo-clad sophisticates in minor roles at Warner Bros. and Columbia before starring in the 1938 serial, *The Great Adventures of Wild Bill Hickok.* As Hickok, Elliott opposed a group of Phantom Raiders who were trying to stop a cattle drive over the Chisholm Trail. A year later he fastened on his guns again, this time to portray the famous scout in *Overland with Kit Carson,* in which he fought a band of Black Raiders headed by a mystery man known as Pegleg. Elliott then made a series of B-Western features for Columbia which kept him busy until he made his final serial, *The Valley of Vanishing Men* (1942) in which he looked for his missing father and broke up the empire of a ruthless slave owner. The next year Elliott moved to Republic where he became one of their most popular players, yet did not appear in any of their serials.

Although Tom Tyler is always considered first as a cowboy star, probably no other sagebrush hero found himself playing such a varied series of serial roles, most of which were non-Western. He was at home in the saddle in *The Phantom of the West* and *Battling with Buffalo Bill,* but he was also a Mountie in *Clancy of the Mounted,* a hunter in *The Jungle Mystery,* a pilot in *The Phantom of*

Left, Sometimes billed as "Wild" Bill Elliott or just William Elliott, this time around he was Bill Elliott and starred with Iris Meredith in *Overland with Kit Carson* (Columbia, 1939). This was Columbia's best Western serial.

177

the Air, and the costumed comic strip hero called *The Phantom.* The role most fans remember him best in was the superhuman star of *Adventures of Captain Marvel.*

Quite a few sagebrush heroes made only a single serial appearance. Tom Mix, probably the most famous cowboy star the screen has ever known (although there are probably more than a few Roy Rogers fans who might disagree), made his final starring screen appearance in Mascot's *The Miracle Rider* (1935). In this tale Tom was a Texas Ranger hot on the trail of the villainous Zaroff (Charles Middleton) who was developing a powerful explosive known as X-94, with which he was terrorizing the Indian population. Tom still rode well, but age was taking its toll and Mix wisely called it a day.

Gene Autry gained instant stardom when he made Mascot's twelve-chapter fantasy serial *Phantom Empire* (1935). *Phantom Empire* found Autry traveling to an underground city called Murania (a table-top miniature fashioned by the Lydecker brothers). After numerous perils, he managed to return safely to his ranch to sing another chorus of "Silver-Haired Daddy of Mine" (which became his first big record hit) after the entire hidden city was melted by a ray.

Ken Maynard had been a tremendous star in silent Westerns, but was pretty much over the hill by the time he made *Mystery Mountain* for Mascot in 1934. He did reasonably well, however, as he sought to uncover a mysterious villain known as The Rattler, who was kept busy committing a series of ruthless murders in order to acquire various land holdings. Tim McCoy was another favorite who had made many big-budget Westerns, but found himself in serials only in the Universal sound-serial debut of *The Indians are Coming* (1929), and the non-Western *Heroes of the Flames* (1931).

One of the real surprises was the serial fate of Bob Steele. Steele was one of the best and most active cowboy stars working. However, when Mascot featured him and fellow Western star Guinn "Big Boy" Williams in a serial, it was the aerial adventure *Mystery Squadron* in which the pair fought a hidden menace called The Black Ace. It was an entertaining vehicle, but if Steele was going to be in only one serial, it should have at least been a Western.

Other popular Western stars who did serial duty included: Allan Lane in *Daredevils of the West,* one of Republic's all-time best action serials; Dick Foran in *Winners of the West* and *Riders of Death Valley;* Donald Barry as Fred Harman's newspaper hero in *Adventures of Red Ryder;* the venerable Harry Carey in *Last of the Mohicans, The Devil Horse* and *The Vanishing Legion;* and Ray "Crash" Corrigan in *The Painted Stallion* and the non-Western *Undersea Kingdom.*

Although Columbia and Universal turned out many satisfactory Western serials, Republic was always the leader in the field. Under directors William Witney, John English, Spencer Bennet and Yakima Canutt, the studio combined all the right ingredients. The camera work by Bud Thackery and Reggie Lanning was exemplary. Musical scores were exciting and pulse-quickening, composed by William Lava, Alberto Columbo, Cy Feuer, and (best of all) Mort Glickman. Set designs were done with painstaking detail and the result was an appearance of expansive interiors (with breakaway props for fight sequences) which contrasted with the cheap, claustrophobic sets at Columbia. I once asked Bud Thackery the secret of Republic's success and he smilingly replied, "undercranking." I think he was right, for the process of undercranking (shooting a film at a few frames slower speed so that the action appears speeded up when the film goes through a projector at normal speed) gave Republic serials and features just that feeling of fast action and excitement that appealed most to the Saturday afternoon crowds.

This expert combination of Republic know-how was put to good use in titles like *Zorro's Fighting Legion, The Painted Stallion, King of the Texas Rangers* (with football great "Slingin' Sammy" Baugh), *Zorro Rides Again, The Lone Ranger* and *The Lone Ranger Rides Again.*

The movie Western has fallen into a period of disinterest, due primarily to over-exposure on television in the fifties and sixties and the lack of any new charismatic stars. Perhaps we have simply become too mature to expect a valiant hero and gallant steed to solve today's more realistic problems.

Top, Johnny Mack Brown lies unconcious as the flames grow near in *The Oregon Trail* (Universal, 1940).

Right, A deadly, if somewhat silly, gantlet of guns was one of the perils faced by Dennis Moore in *Raiders of Ghost City* (Universal, 1944).

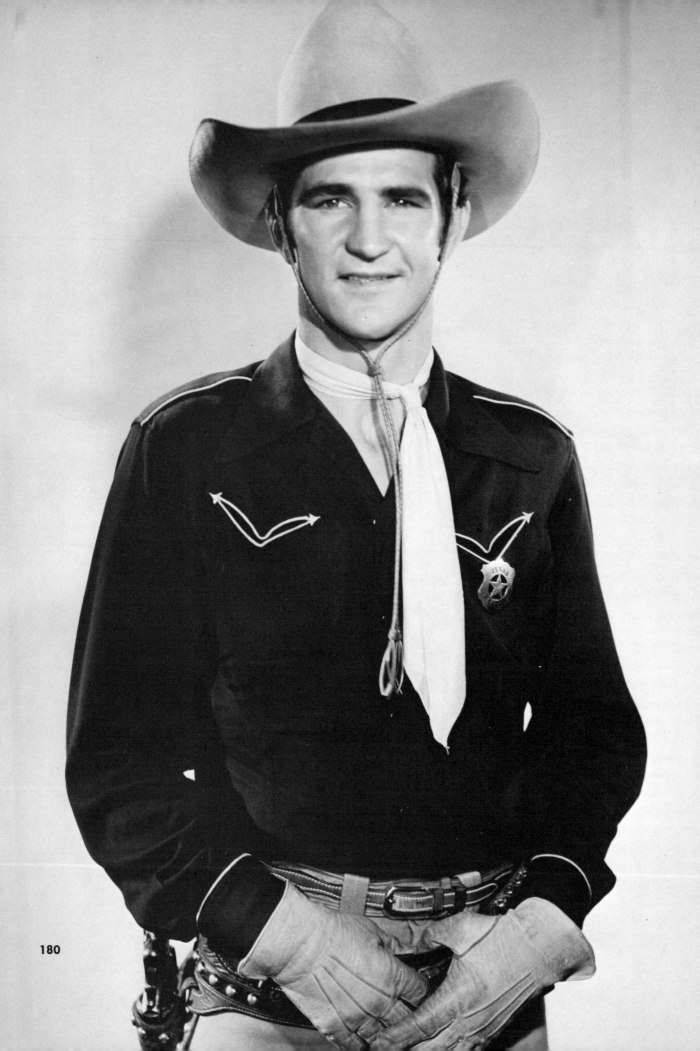

Left, "Slingin' Sammy" Baugh, an All-American football star, looked great but acted poorly in *King of the Texas Rangers* (Republic, 1941).

Above, In a publicity shot "Slingin' Sammy" Baugh tosses the ball to Vera Hruba Ralston during a break from *King of the Texas Rangers* (Republic, 1941). Ralston was filming *Ice Capades* at the time.

NAT LEVINE presents

THE MIGHTIEST OF WESTERN STARS

Ken Maynard

with HIS WONDER HORSE "TARZAN"

in

"MYSTERY MOUNTAIN"

with an All-Star Cast

DIRECTED *by* OTTO BROWER *and* B. REEVES EASON

A *Mascot Master Serial*

MASCOT SERIALS

"BLAZING THE TRA...

IN TWELVE SMASHING, ACTION-LOADED CHAPTERS

Left, Dick Foran was a very likable hero in *Winners of the West* (Universal, 1940).

Bottom, Ray Corrigan and Julia Thayer strike a romantic, though strictly publicity, pose for *The Painted Stallion* (Republic, 1937).

182

Right, A masked Paul Guilfoyle confronts Victoria Horne in *The Scarlet Horseman* (Universal, 1946).

Below, Tom Mix appeared in his last film and only serial when he made *The Miracle Rider* (Mascot, 1935).

Above, Clayton Moore glamorized Jesse James when he appeared in *Adventures of Frank and Jesse James* (Republic, 1948). In this scene he and Noel Neill try to get a little information from Tom Steele.

Left, Peggy Stewart is rescued by a masked Robert Kent in *The Phantom Rider* (Republic, 1946).

Right, Clayton Moore's first appearance as Jesse James was with Linda Stirling in *Jesse James Rides Again* (Republic, 1947).

Below, Gene Autry experiments with a Muranian robot in *Phantom Empire* (Mascot, 1935). This serial launched Autry on his spectacular Western career after he had appeared briefly in two other Mascot films.

Left, In *The Valley of Vanishing Men* (Columbia, 1942) Bill Elliott matched wits and fists with I. Stanford Jolley.

Above, An early morning crew, well-protected from the cold, prepares to shoot a scene for *Daredevils of the West* (Republic, 1943). Kay Aldridge and Joe Yrigoyen are on the stage and George J. Lewis is on horseback under the mike boom.

Right, One of the guiding forces at Universal was producer/director Henry MacRae. Here, in a publicity still for *Wild West Days* (Universal, 1937) he is surrounded by his script girl, Johnny Mack Brown, Frank McGlynn, Jr. and Bob McClung.

Top left, Allan Lane is about to meet a fiery death in a volcanic pit in this chapter ending from *Daredevils of the West* (Republic, 1943).

Below, veteran Western star Buck Jones gets the drop on Al Ferguson in *White Eagle* (Columbia, 1941).

Top right, Johnny Mack Brown and Robert Kortman escape a deadly trap in *Wild West Days* (Universal, 1937).

Below, Roy Barcroft looks like he's about to finish off Richard Powers (who also used the names of Tom Keene and George Duryea) in *Desperadoes of the West* (Republic, 1950).

Top left, Keith Richards was Jesse James and Noel Neill his female support in *The James Brothers of Missouri* (Republic, 1950).

Bottom left, Harry Cording and Charles Stevens have Lon Chaney, Jr. at a disadvantage in *Overland Mail* (Universal, 1942).

Above, Buck Jones is behind that mask as *The Phantom Rider* (Universal, 1936) metes out justice.

Left, Adele Jergens and Robert Scott were the likable leads in *Black Arrow* (Columbia, 1944).

14 HOMEFRONT HEROES

WAR MAY, INDEED, be hell, but to the millions of kids who flocked to matinees to see the serials during World War II, it was a time of tremendous enthusiasm and excitement. Our wartime screen heroes were no longer fighting a few demented villains bent on acquiring personal wealth or power, but a parade of malevolent Axis agents who were out to take over America and control our very lives. As one, we applauded each enemy failure and screamed our approval as these treacherous devils were punished for their crimes with swift (and usually violent) death.

Studio-created pyrotechnics were the visual stimulants that made these serials so thrilling as our eyes were dazzled by a seemingly endless parade of warehouses being blown up, cars exploding, and planes plunging to thunderous conflagrations. Republic was the best-equipped studio to handle this type of production. Their excellent special-effects department headed by Howard and Theodore Lydecker created minatures that were vastly superior to those being done by the major producing companies. Their secret was in building large-scale (as opposed to tabletop) models and shooting them outside against natural backgrounds, using daylight instead of harsh studio lights.

Republic began its battle against enemy villainy with *Spy Smasher,* a 1942 adventure starring Kane Richmond as the costumed comic-book hero who battled a Nazi menace called The Mask. With stuntman David Sharpe doubling for Richmond in the action sequences, *Spy Smasher* was filled with acrobatic fight sequences and inventive chapter endings which found our hero being trapped in a tunnel by burning oil, threatened by drowning in a flooded submarine compartment, and nearly being cremated in a pottery kiln. Unlike the comic strip, Republic screenwriters gave Spy Smasher a twin brother, forcing Richmond to work twice as hard in a dual role. It was done for a legitimate purpose, however—in Chapter Eleven one brother sacrificed his life for the other. Wartime morality demanded this kind of unselfish sacrifice, and we found this recurring theme appear in numerous other serials. Hans Schumm's portrayal of The Mask was the first in a long line of stereotypes which pictured hard-faced Nazis as propagandizing tyrants.

All three Axis powers were equally represented in *King of the Mounties,* another 1942 Republic presentation. Allan Lane, one of the studio's more capable leading men, had scored a personal success in 1940 in *King of the Royal Mounted,* and this sequel found him battling America's foes in top style. In a cleverly-devised plot, the villains operated from the inside of a volcano, access to which was only obtained by flying a "Bat Plane" which had the ability to descend directly into the mouth of the crater. In a spectacular finale, Lane managed to gain access to the hidden headquarters and, after dropping bombs into the belching lava, escaped just as the enemy and the volcano were engulfed in explosions.

Rod Cameron was an excellent choice to play Rex Bennett, a government man on the trail of Japanese saboteurs in *G-Men vs. the Black Dragon.* Tall and athletic, Cameron was able to throw the most convincing punches of any serial hero, and *G-Men vs. the Black Dragon* had some of the most extensively-choreographed fight sequences of any Republic serial filmed up to that time. Nino Pipitone was creatively evil as the sinister Haruchi, smuggled into the United States in a mummy case and in a state of suspended animation. Two all-time favorite chapter endings were the sequence in which a series of transmission towers were being blown up as Cameron battled an agent on top of one, and a clever trap in which the heroine (Constance Worth) was tied to a chair directly in the path of a deadly spear which would eventually be released when the miniature spears held by two revolving figurines touched.

The success of *G-Men vs. the Black Dragon* brought a sequel the same year with Cameron again playing Rex Bennett in *Secret Service in Darkest Africa.* Having successfully thwarted the Japanese, it was time to tackle the Nazis who were out to take over Africa as a stepping stone to world conquest. Like its predecessor, this serial was similarly full of explosive endings and fight sequences in which entire rooms were literally torn apart.

Republic's final fling at wartime heroics was *The Masked Marvel,* in which Tom Steele (the studio's hardest-working stuntman) took twelve chapters to uncover the evil machinations of a Japanese agent called Sakima, and

Left, this bit of action by Rod Cameron, masquerading as a German agent, was bound to bring prolonged shouting and applause from young audiences who watched *Secret Service in Darkest Africa* (Republic, 1943).

didn't even get credit on the screen for his work. Although Steele did all the action work and wore the hero's mask, supposedly The Marvel was one of four insurance investigators (portrayed by four terrible actors who deserve no mention here) who were assigned to break up a sabotage ring. The ending of Chapter One in which a huge gas storage tank explodes while The Marvel and enemy agents are fighting on top remains one of the Lydecker's best miniature sequences.

By the time World War II was half-over Universal Pictures was entering the last phase of its serial-producing reign which had started back in the silent era. Handicapped by cheap sets, unimaginative plots and the use of newsreel footage rather than good miniatures, Universal failed to generate much excitement with its wartime serial product. *Don Winslow of the Navy* and *Don Winslow of the Coast Guard,* both starring Don Terry as the naval hero who appeared both on radio and in comics, had some merit. Winslow was up against a Nazi terrorist called The Scorpion in both serials. In the 1945 version of *Secret Agent X-9,* based on the character created by Alex Raymond for the comics, Lloyd Bridges found himself battling enemy agents with the able assistance of Keye Luke (taking time off from playing Charlie Chan's Number One Son). *Adventures of Smilin' Jack,* with young Tom Brown as the energetic lead, had a superb cast composed of old reliables like Sidney Toler, Edgar Barrier, Rose Hobart and Turhan Bey, but was routinely scripted. For one chapter ending the studio used the complete and elaborately-staged plane crash from Alfred Hitchcock's classic *Foreign Correspondent.*

Other Universal titles like *Sea Raiders, Sky Raiders, Adventures of the Flying Cadets, Junior G-Men* and *Junior G-Men of the Air* had the casting assistance of youthful favorites like The East Side Kids, The Dead End Kids and The Little Tough Guys (could anyone ever tell who belonged to which group?) but the end results were inconsequential affairs that gave the viewer little to get excited about.

Over at Columbia war was definitely fun as the studio writers and directors gave us several items which pictured our deadly adversaries as bumbling incompetents. In *Captain Midnight* (another radio and comic book favorite brought to cinema life) Dave O'Brien matched wits with a forever ranting and raving James Craven as the latter sought to obtain secret bombsights and destroy our ace of the airways. In *The Secret Code,* Paul Kelly masqueraded as The Black Commando in order to break up a gang of Nazi saboteurs. His partner, Clancy Cooper, was constantly labeling the enemy agents as "Ratzis" and Kelly was always shown to have his fingers crossed when forced to salute a picture of Hitler. At the end of each episode of *The Secret Code* Selmer Jackson, who seemed to make a career out of playing army officers and who narrated a great many training films for the Armed Forces, gave audiences a lesson in how to break various codes. The lessons seemed to get sillier as each week went by with Jackson spelling out a group of letters and advising us with a straight face that "this is clearly a word."

For unadulterated lunacy, however, it is hard to top *Batman.* J. Carrol Naish, a really first-rate character actor, portrayed a Japanese agent called Dr. Daka in such an idiotic fashion that only the most naive viewer could stop himself from laughing the minute Naish opened his mouth. Headquartered in an old arcade attraction supposedly showing the horrors of enemy torture, Dr. Daka had a laboratory filled with electrical devices including a weird helmet in which he converted his enemies into zombie-like slaves. He was at his best when he was feeding the pet alligators which he kept in a pit, ever-at-the-ready for his victims. One scene found him tossing meat into the pit and then asking the alligators if they wanted something more as he slyly glanced at the leg of a zombie standing next to him. It somehow seemed only right that Dr. Daka himself would end up in that pit in Chapter Fifteen. As Batman, Lewis Wilson wasn't much easier to take as he wore a loose-fitting outfit that always seemed to sag and was frequently having trouble looking correctly through the eye slits in his cowl. Columbia serials were made in a light-hearted vein, for laughs and entertainment as opposed to the more plot-heavy Universal efforts and the action-packed Republic product, but *Batman* stretched our tolerance level a bit too much.

By the end of 1945 World War II was over, and serial scriptwriters breathed a collective sigh of relief as they went back to giving us more mundane predators in the guise of mad scientists, hooded horrors and other more recognizable matinee villains.

Right, while Rod Cameron fights off an ax-wielding George J. Lewis, his Chinese-American partner Roland Got grabs a piece of Noel Cravat's face in *G-Men vs. The Black Dragon* (Republic, 1943).

Below, Philip Ahn looks on approvingly as Sidney Toler scans an important map given to him by Tom Brown in *Adventures of Smilin' Jack* (Universal, 1943).

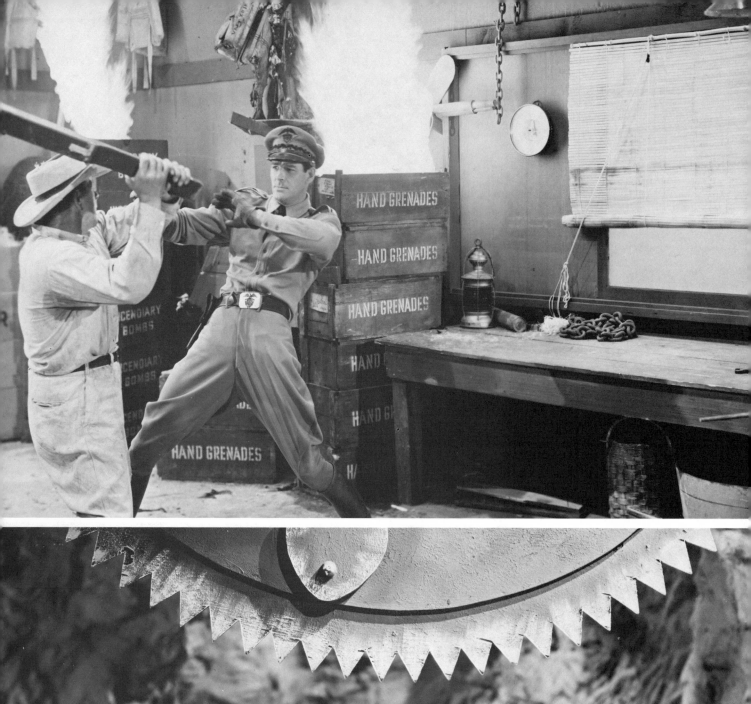

Top left, Rod Cameron battles Duke Green while the burning grenades threaten to blow them both to pieces in *Secret Service in Darkest Africa* (Republic, 1943).

Bottom left, Rod Cameron faces elaborate execution in *Secret Service in Darkest Africa* (Republic, 1943).

Below, Universal updated *Secret Agent X-9* (Universal, 1945) and had Keye Luke and Lloyd Bridges fighting Nazi agents.

UNCLE SAM'S SECRET AGENTS BATTLE NAZI SPIES IN A BLOOD-TINGLING CHAPTER PLAY

THE SECRET-CODE

A great serial thriller!

Chapter 1 "ENEMY PASSPORT"

with

PAUL KELLY • ANNE NAGEL

Original screen play by Basil Dickey, Leighton Brill, Robert Beche

Directed by SPENCER G. BENNET

A COLUMBIA CHAPTER PLAY

COLUMBIA PICTURES

Right, Tom Steele is behind the mask and battling fellow stuntman Dale Van Sickel in *The Masked Marvel* (Republic, 1943).

Below, the shattering finale of Chapter One of *The Masked Marvel* (Republic, 1943) found our hero and this gas tank being blown to bits (in miniature special effects, naturally).

Above, Jennifer Holt and Johnny Downs survive another peril in *Adventures of the Flying Cadets* (Universal, 1943). Jennifer was Jack Holt's daughter and Tim Holt's sister, forming a talented family acting triumvirate.

Left, this unlikely trio of Milburn Stone, Edgar Kennedy and Joseph Crehan were the heroes of *Mystery of the River Boat* (Universal, 1944).

199

Right, Don Terry, star of *Don Winslow of the Navy* (Universal, 1941), takes a glance at the proofsheet of his comic strip counterpart.

Below, a year later Don Terry and Walter Sande switched services in *Don Winslow of the Coast Guard* (Universal, 1943).

Far right, Walter Sande and Don Terry escape a destructive explosion in *Don Winslow of the Navy* (Universal, 1942).

Above, Lionel Atwill gave a demeaning portrayal of The Baron in *Junior G-Men of the Air* (Universal, 1942).

Right, J. Carrol Naish was an outlandish Japanese agent in *Batman* (Columbia, 1943).

Right, Allan Lane used the enemies' Falcon airship to invade their secret volcanic base in *King of the Mounties* (Republic, 1942).

Below, Billy Halop, Huntz Hall, Gabriel Dell, Bernard Punsley and Frank Albertson joined together to fight the Axis in *Junior G-Men of the Air* (Universal, 1942).

IN ORDER TO give audiences a welcome respite from Western and contemporary themes, the serial producers occasionally included a jungle adventure in their shooting schedules. Most of the time these animal thrillers were little more than embellished Westerns using traditional ranch locations in the Hollywood area and sparsely-decorated back lot sets. In order to give these films some semblance of reality, studios would hire a few pet animals and frequently used stock footage clips from earlier jungle travelogues showing charging lions and assorted savage animal battles.

Mascot went on a cinema safari three times with their productions of *King of the Kongo, King of the Wild* and *The Lost Jungle.* Only the last of the trio had any real merit. Clyde Beatty had achieved the reputation of being the greatest animal trainer alive. He wasn't much of an actor, but the script of *The Lost Jungle* only required that he play himself in an adventure which found him searching for a lost professor in an uncharted island jungle. Also in the cast of *The Lost Jungle* was a young boy who would go on to enormous screen success—Mickey Rooney. Another actor whose career was about to ascend rapidly was given fifth billing in *King of the Wild*—Boris Karloff. After Karloff appeared in *Frankenstein,* re-issues of *King of the Wild* gave him top-billing over the serial's real stars, Walter Miller and Nora Lane.

Independent producers also sought to cash in at the box office with jungle adventures and the results were mixed. *Tarzan, the Fearless,* with Buster Crabbe as an inarticulate Ape Man, had a few thrills, but Herman Brix fared much better as the lead in *The New Adventures of Tarzan,* which was shot on location in Guatemala. Two of the worst serials ever made both turned out to be set in jungle locales: *Queen of the Jungle* starring Mary Kornman (shot on a tiny studio set, these scenes then being interwoven with stock from the much more elaborately staged silent serial, *The Jungle Goddess);* and *The Lost City* (even the talents of star Kane Richmond couldn't overcome the silliness of a plot which found an over-emoting William "Stage" Boyd creating an army of giant black slaves). Although *The Return of Chandu (The Magician)* took place on an island, it should be included in this group

because it did possess many of the genre's basic ingredients (high priests, savage tribes, etc.) and it did boast a superlative performance by Bela Lugosi as Chandu, making the film the best of the independent releases.

Universal began their jungle adventures in 1929 with Frank Merrill starring as *Tarzan, the Tiger* in a story dealing with jewel thieves. Three years later in *The Jungle Mystery,* star Tom Tyler was also after thieves, but this time their object was ivory. Subsequent Universal offerings included: *Perils of Pauline,* with Evalyn Knapp playing the intrepid heroine who was trying to protect an important invention created by her scientist father; *Pirate Treasure,* with daredevil stunt ace Richard Talmadge trying to find a treasure buried by one of his piratical ancestors; *The Call of the Savage,* with young Noah Berry, Jr. portraying "Jan of the Jungle" in a story which started out in traditional jungle fashion, but ended in the discovery of the lost kingdom of Mu, where our hero faced more mechanized perils (i.e., a room in which a ceiling full of spikes slowly descended upon him); and *Jungle Jim,* in which Grant Withers played Alex Raymond's famous comic strip character in a story that found Jim out to protect a jungle white girl who was really the heir to a fabulous fortune. Universal's final jungle serial of the thirties was the popular *Tim Tyler's Luck,* starring Frankie Thomas as the young hero created by Lyman Young for the Sunday newspapers. Tim was in Africa to search for his lost father, but always lurking behind him was his notorious adversary, Spider Webb (Norman Willis), who was also after the elder Tyler and a hidden cache of ivory. It was colorful, inventive fun and the action was backed up by an excellent musical score that was used in many other Universal serials and features. The studio concluded its jungle meanderings with *Jungle Queen* in 1945 and *Lost City of the Jungle* the following year. *Jungle Queen* featured soon-to-become-a-star Ruth Roman as a jungle ruler who always came to the rescue of stars Edward Norris and Eddie Quillan just in time to save them from deadly lions, deadlier natives or just plain raging infernos. As Lothel, Roman had the ability to walk through flames without injury, and she demonstrated this to her followers, as well as to the audience, with boring regularity. *Lost City of the*

Left, The Tiger Woman (Republic, 1944) was the first of six serials starring former model Linda Stirling.

Jungle found Lionel Atwill out to acquire "Meteorium 245," a supposed defense against atomic bombs, but Russell Hayden and Keye Luke quickly put an end to his mad endeavors after thirteen weekly episodes.

Columbia began that studio's twenty-year-long string of serials with *Jungle Menace*. Cast in the lead was the famous animal hunter and trainer, Frank Buck. Unfortunately, Buck was no actor, and had little to do except engage in a few animal sequences. Most of the film featured LeRoy Mason and William Bakewell doing battle over the rights to a rubber planatation. It was probably Columbia's dullest serial adventure—a typical chapter ending was the firing of a shot through a window which killed the elder owner of the plantation. Three years later Columbia gave us a much more exciting and humorous film when *Terry and the Pirates* was brought to the screen. Director James W. Horne found it impossible to do a straight serial without having his actors "ham" up their dialogue and overreact (as though they were in a silent movie) with exaggerated gestures. With young William Tracy as Terry, Granville Owen as Pat Ryan, and Joyce Bryant as Normandie, *Terry and the Pirates* was another tale of a party in search of a lost civilization. Columbia's remaining jungle serials included: *The Phantom,* in which Tom Tyler was the comic strip hero who prevented the secret treasure in a lost city from being stolen; *Jungle Raiders,* with Kane Richmond as a doctor trying to heal the natives and protect them from enemies after (yet another) secret treasure; *Congo Bill,* with Don McGuire as the comic book hero trying to acquire for the amply proportioned Cleo Moore a letter proving she was the heir to a fortune; *King of the Congo,* with Buster Crabbe in his final serial role disposing of a band of enemy agents; and, finally, *Adventures of Captain Africa* with John Hart trying to protect a caliph's throne from some very intimidating usurpers.

Republic also began its twenty-year run of serials with a jungle story, the 1936 production of *Darkest Africa.* With Clyde Beatty once again playing himself, *Darkest Africa* was an inventive film that featured a lost city ruled by a despot who had at his disposal (among other things) a band of flying Bat Men, whose flying sequences were cleverly-staged and provided a preview of similar action staged in *Adventures of Captain Marvel* five years later. In 1941 Republic gave audiences the best of all the jungle serials produced, *Jungle Girl.* With Frances Gifford por-

traying Nyoka, Tom Neal as hero Jack Stanton, and Trevor Bardette and Gerald Mohr as their adversaries, *Jungle Girl* was replete with thrilling climaxes as the opposing sides fought for a fortune in diamonds. With both Helen Thurston and David Sharpe doing her stunt work, Gifford swung through the trees with the skill of Tarzan, leaped from cliffs into alligator-filled lakes, battled quicksand and poison gas, finally emerging victorious after fifteen memorable episodes. *Jungle Girl* was followed a year later by *Perils of Nyoka* with Kay Aldridge now playing the jungle heroine and with Clayton Moore as her very capable defender. Another fifteen-chapter serial, *Perils of Nyoka,* found our champions after some long-lost secret tablets that held the cure for cancer. In addition, the tablets also contained directions to a secret treasure sought unsuccessfully by the evil Vultura (Lorna Gray). Although *Perils of Nyoka* was exciting, Aldridge could not quite match up to Gifford in the role of Nyoka, and most of the action was left to Moore.

Although Republic's *Secret Service in Darkest Africa* and *The Tiger Woman* were ostensibly jungle stories, both looked as if they had been shot on a ranch. *Secret Service in Darkest Africa* was a straight action yarn that found Rod Cameron battling a bunch of Nazi agents who kept trying to blow him up in trap after trap; *The Tiger Woman* featured the serial debut of Republic's new action queen, Linda Stirling, in a tale which found her and Allan Lane trying to prevent villain LeRoy Mason from getting secret papers proving The Tiger Woman to be the heiress to a fortune. Fetchingly clad, Stirling was excellent in her role, and *The Tiger Woman* remains her best-remembered adventure.

Republic's final jungle treks were the simply awful *Jungle Drums of Africa* (made in 1953 with Clayton Moore as a uranium mining engineer), and *Panther Girl of the Congo* (with Phyllis Coates dressed to match stock footage featuring Frances Gifford from *Jungle Girl).* A science-fiction element was added to the standard jungle fare here as The Panther Girl found herself fighting giant claw monsters (crayfish in miniature sets with a giant claw for an occasional close-up) created by a villainous doctor (Arthur Space) who had developed a special hormone to enlarge the devilish crustaceans. *Panther Girl of the Congo* and *King of the Carnival* (both made in 1955) were Republic's final presentations to Saturday matinee regulars.

Noah Beery, Jr. was Jan of the Jungle in *The Call of the Savage* (Universal, 1935). Dorothy Short was the damsel in distress this time around.

Famous animal hunter Frank Buck lent his presence to Columbia's first serial, *Jungle Menace* (Columbia, 1937), but what little action transpired was carried on by LeRoy Mason and others.

Clyde Beatty had a chance to demonstrate his animal training techniques in *The Lost Jungle* (Mascot, 1934).

Ruth Roman strikes a rather aloof pose as the *Jungle Queen* (Universal, 1945).

Left, Clayton Moore and Phyllis Coates were the stars of Republic's dullest and most uninteresting serial, *Jungle Drums of Africa* (Republic, 1953).

Below, Handsome Kane Richmond found himself at odds with Veda Ann Borg in *Jungle Raiders* (Columbia, 1945).

Bottom, The costumed Bat Men seem to have Clyde Beatty and young Manuel King at their mercy in Republic Pictures' first serial venture, *Darkest Africa* (Republic, 1936).

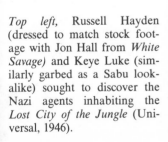

Top left, Russell Hayden (dressed to match stock footage with Jon Hall from *White Savage)* and Keye Luke (similarly garbed as a Sabu lookalike) sought to discover the Nazi agents inhabiting the *Lost City of the Jungle* (Universal, 1946).

Bottom left, flanked by Frank Lackteen and Noah Beery, Jr., Tom Tyler sets out to solve *The Jungle Mystery* (Universal, 1932).

Right, Frances Gifford finally uncovers the villainy of Gerald Mohr in *Jungle Girl* (Republic, 1941).

Below, Helen Thurston is doubling for Frances Gifford on the altar, while witch-doctor Frank Lackteen prepares to feed her into the deadly flames, in this scene from *Jungle Girl* (Republic, 1941).

"PERILS OF NYOKA"

A REPUBLIC SERIAL 15 CHAPTERS

Chapter 4 ASCENDING DOOM

Left, Kay Aldridge is appropriately menaced by Emil Van Horn inside Satan's gorilla skin in *Perils of Nyoka* (Republic, 1942).

212

Right, Kay Aldridge looks through some film clips with veteran cameraman Reggie Lanning on the set of *Perils of Nyoka* (Republic, 1942).

Below, Director William Witney puts Lorna Gray and Kay Aldridge through their paces in *Perils of Nyoka* (Republic, 1942).

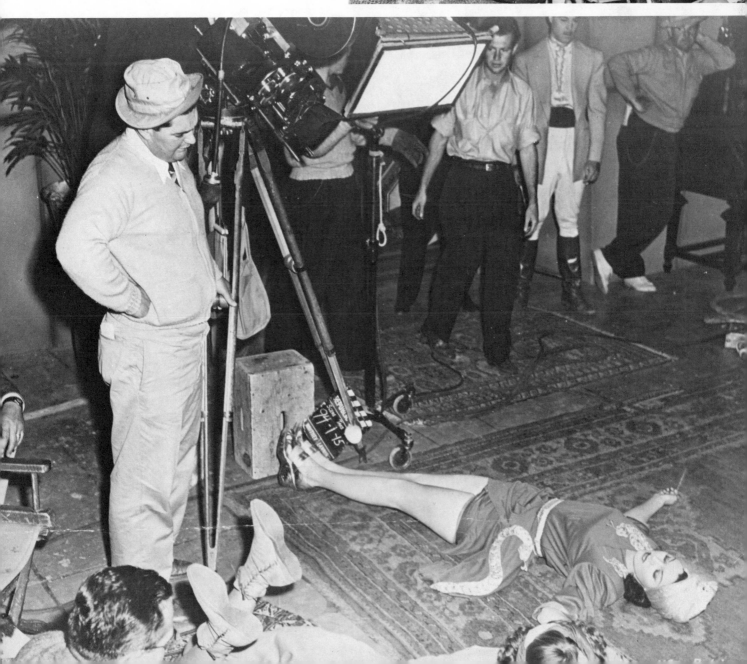

Above, Linda Stirling and Allan Lane try to get a little information from George J. Lewis and stuntman Duke Green in *The Tiger Woman* (Republic, 1944).

Right, Frank Lackteen is up to his usual skullduggery as he menaces Evalyn Knapp in *Perils of Pauline* (Universal, 1934).

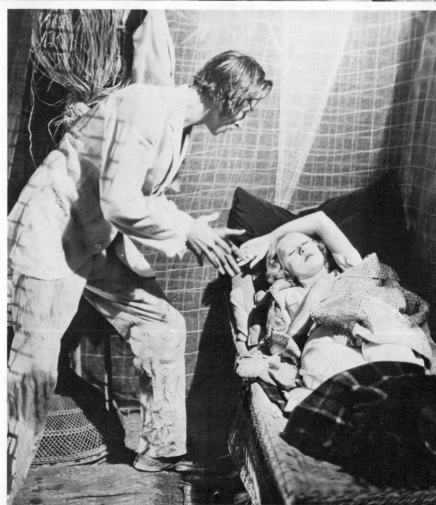

HORROR STALKS THE JUNGLE!

THE MOST EXCITING SERIAL EVER FILMED!

PANTHER GIRL OF THE KONGO

A REPUBLIC SERIAL IN 12 CHAPTERS

FEATURING
PHYLLIS COATES · MYRON HEALEY
ARTHUR SPACE · JOHN DAY · MIKE RAGAN

Written by RONALD DAVIDSON · Associate Producer-Director FRANKLIN ADREON
REPUBLIC PICTURES CORPORATION—HERBERT J. YATES, President

MUCH OF THE FUN derived from weekly attendance at the serials was due in no small degree to our bigger-than-life heroes' battles with a seemingly endless parade of grotesquely-clad scoundrels. These masked devils, with their secret laboratories full of death-dealing gadgetry and apparent disdain for human life, were like magnets drawing us back week after week to see if our powers of deduction were superior to the leading man's in determining the identity of the real culprits. We were usually wrong, of course, but what did that matter? The real thrills were in the chase, not the capture. The formula was a standard one: three to five members of a council (or board of directors or some similar group) outwardly opposed to the villainy transpiring, but harboring one among them who led a malevolent double life. There were seldom any logical clues given to help uncover the man behind the mask. Indeed, most of the time someone else's voice was used and, more often than not, stuntmen wore the outfits to save producers the cost of hiring another actor until he was needed for the unmasking scene in the last chapter.

It is difficult to get serial fans to agree on a choice for a favorite masked villain. The list of contenders was large and varied, offering something to please almost every taste. My personal choice was always that of the mysterious Scorpion in *Adventures of Captain Marvel*. The Scorpion was out to dominate the world by controlling the destructive powers harnessed in a strange device known as the "Golden Scorpion Atom Smasher." All that was needed was a series of lenses which fit into this contraption. Naturally, the lenses were divided among the film's group of suspects and we only discovered who The Scorpion was after he had eliminated all his companions.

The Lightning in *Fighting Devil Dogs* had developed an electronic firebolt which he unleased upon his hapless victims, electrocuting them *en masse*. Cloaked in a satin-finished outfit with a flowing cape and face-concealing helmet, The Lightning was an imposing agent of destruction and kept Lee Powell and Herman Brix, two marines on his trail, guessing as to whether he might be the gardener, the servant, the lab assistant or any of several others in their group of suspects. The Lightning also had the advantage of operating from a studio-created airship

called "The Wing" (which had been designed earlier for the *Dick Tracy* serial).

The Crimson Ghost hid his identity behind a ghoulish skeleton-faced mask and hoped to rule the world by controlling a machine called a "cyclotrode." One of the means by which he was able to enlist the aid of his enemies was by placing a "control collar" around their necks through which he could transmit instructions. Removal of the collar brought about instant death. One chapter ending found the hero (Charles Quigley) trying frantically to remove a collar from the neck of his co-star (Linda Stirling) without killing her.

With his ability to become invisible by means of a special machine, The Ghost in *Dick Tracy vs. Crime, Inc,* had a definite advantage over his pursuers, but that didn't prevent Ralph Byrd from tracking him down by means of dogs and special tricks. The Ghost, unlike most of his ilk who lusted after wealth and power, had revenge driving him as he sought to eliminate those who had sent his brother to prison. Instead of victory, however, The Ghost's final reward was electrocution in a last chapter labeled "Retribution."

Dr. Vulcan's "Decimator" in *King of the Rocket Men* looked suspiciously like The Crimson Ghost's "Cyclotrode" of a few years earlier, and its purpose was the same, to dominate mankind. He didn't succeed completely, but he did manage to destroy, via stock footage from an earlier feature, a good many ships and buildings in New York Harbor. He met an explosive fate when a group of army planes dropped a load of bombs on his island retreat.

Anyone who couldn't guess the identity of Pegleg in *Overland With Kit Carson* should have his popcorn taken away. Even a hideous scar and a fake missing limb couldn't conceal the actor who played the role. They did try, though! They gave him a beard and a French accent in his role as one of the suspects, but most kids were smart enough to see through those red herring devices, as was Bill Elliott when he finally forced Pegleg into a situation where he was trampled to death by a horse that he had trained to be a killer.

Not all the mystery men were evil. In *Daredevils of the Red Circle,* The Red Circle kept writing notes to the three

The Scorpion, featured in *Adventures of Captain Marvel* (Republic, 1941), sought world domination by controlling an atom-smashing device. Most serial buffs choose The Scorpion as their favorite serial villain.

daredevil circus stars to warn them of various perils as they sought to uncover the mysterious 39013, played by Charles Middleton. *The Green Archer* also had a colorful title character who came to the frequent aid of star Victor Jory, even though a bogus Green Archer would pop up from time to time to confuse viewers.

The famed pulp hero, The Spider, had two mystery men to deal with in his pair of serial adventures. In *The Spider's Web* it was The Octopus who sought to wrap his human tentacles around a city which cowered beneath his savage onslaughts against industry. With his fake hand resting on the desk, we knew he would dispense sudden death quickly from a hidden gun-clenching hand under his robe, to any henchman who failed to follow his orders. We were less impressed by The Gargoyle in *The Spider Returns.* With his arms flailing wildly and the repeated temper tantrems he directed at his bungling band of helpers, he cut a sorry figure as a villain.

More to our liking was Captain Mephisto in *Manhunt of Mystery Island.* Portrayed by veteran badman Roy Barcroft, Mephisto was the reincarnation of an ancestor of the four owners of Mystery Island. By means of a transformation chair, one of the four is able to redesign the molecular structure of his body so that he resembles the ancient pirate. Mephisto's main interest lay in forcing a scientist to perfect and build a large-scale model of a device called a "radiatomic power transmitter," a machine which could control world transportation networks. Mephisto was at his evil best when he was luring hero Richard Bailey and heroine Linda Stirling into such diverse traps as a flooding mine tunnel, a crushing wine press, volcanic craters, and a plunging suspension bridge.

Although Don Del Oro, the helmeted heavy of *Zorro's Fighting Legion,* was the most famous Western-oriented mystery man, there were several other favorites that demanded some recognition: The Rattler, who took cowboy star Ken Maynard to task in *Mystery Mountain;* The Wolf Man in *The Lightning Warrior* and The Skull in *Deadwood Dick.*

Many of the comic strip serials also featured colorful opponents for our heroes to fight. *Batman and Robin* were after The Wizard and the remote-control machine in his possession. *Bruce Gentry* found his hands full trying to prevent The Recorder from unleashing a deadly barrage of electrically-controlled flying discs upon chosen targets (the discs appeared as cartoon drawings in this cheap Columbia production). Even radio's *The Shadow* almost met his match on screen as he battled another invisible foe, The Black Tiger and *Mandrake, the Magician* just barely outwitted The Wasp.

On and on they came. *The Iron Claw* and *The Clutching Hand,* with the hideous shadows of their deformed appendages playing on the walls of castles and cabins as their owners slinked through secret passageways and hidden doors. The menaces who tried to get John Wayne: The Eagle in *The Shadow of the Eagle,* The Wrecker in *Hurricane Express* and El Shaitan in *The Three Musketeers.* The Tiger Shark who, operating from his secret island, gave the *Fighting Marines* quite a chase. The Black Ace with his devastating attacks against Bob Steele in *Mystery Squadron.* The Dragon, who sent his messages via prayer-wheels and who almost crushed *Ace Drummond* in a room where the walls closed. The Voice in *Government Agents vs. Phantom Legion* who was waging war against the public highway transportation system, and, to conclude only a partial listing, The Black Knight, a troublemaker who gave King Arthur's Round Table nothing but problems in *Adventures of Sir Galahad.*

The only redeeming feature of this entire collection of incredible malcontents was that we had the pleasure of watching their machinations destroy them one by one. And it was a pleasure, for, bad as they were, they taught a generation of youngsters (admittedly in an over-simplified manner) the folly of evil. The serial fan looks back with fond memories of the days when all he had to worry about was an occasional Scorpion or Clutching Hand who merely wanted to rule the world.

Right, The Gargoyle gives a typical Columbia Pictures reaction in *The Spider Returns* (Columbia, 1941).

Below, The Ghost, with the capable help of John Davidson as Lucifer, gave his adversary, Dick Tracy enough trouble to fill fifteen episodes in *Dick Tracy vs. Crime, Inc.* (Republic, 1941). Through a mysterious machine and a disc worn around his neck, he had the ability to render himself invisible.

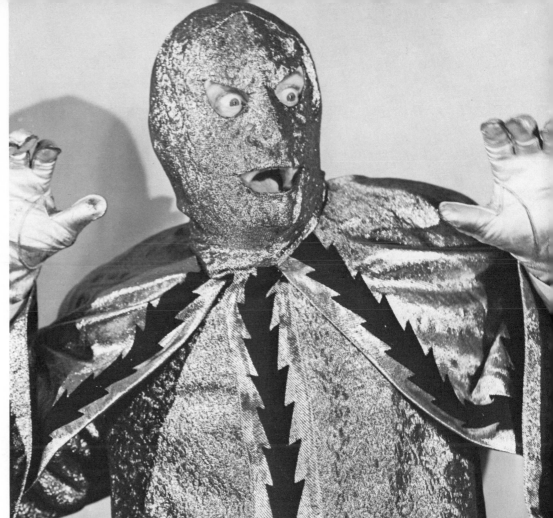

Right, Up to a point, no one knew for sure whether *The Green Arch*(Columbia, 1940) was friend or foe. This was another serial which wa done also as an early silent adventure.

Above, The mysterious Pegleg was as deadly with a knife as a gun in *Overland with Kit Carson* (Columbia, 1939).

Right, Wartime villainy lurks behind the mask of The Black Hangman in *Adventures of the Flying Cadets* (Universal, 1943).

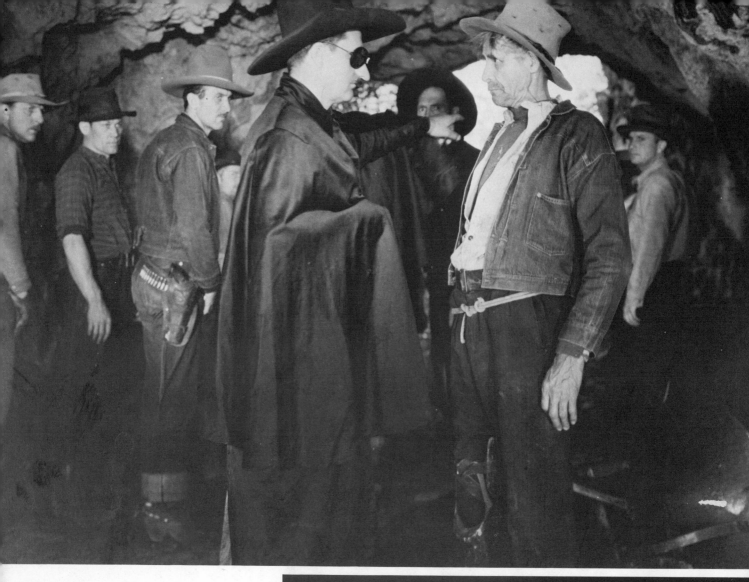

Above, In *Mystery Mountain* (Mascot, 1934) it was the mysterious Rattler who gave orders to his band of killers.

Right, The Wasp forced *Mandrake, the Magician* (Columbia, 1939) to use every trick at his disposal.

222

Left, Roy Barcroft portrayed the reincarnated pirate Captain Mephisto in *Manhunt of Mystery Island* (Republic, 1945). In reality, Mephisto was one of four owners of the island, one of whom went through a molecular structure change in a transformation chair.

Below, The Wizard, assisted by Greg McClure, gave a hard time to *Batman and Robin* (Columbia, 1949).

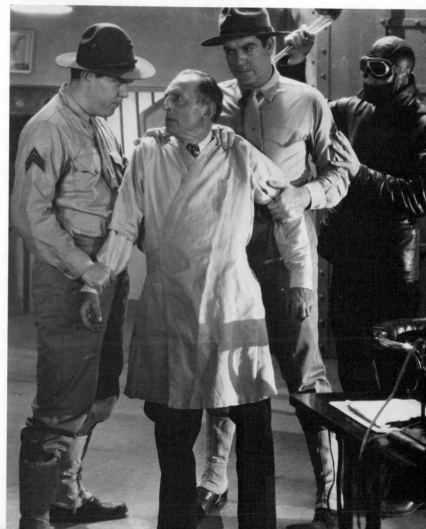

Above, Could that possibly be a woman under the robes of *The Master Key* (Universal, 1945)? Her chief henchman, Addison Richards, has just gunned down another enemy.

Right, As Adrian Morris and Grant Withers forcibly question Frank Reicher in *Fighting Marines* (Mascot, 1935), the masked Tiger Shark enters the scene.

Far right, The Iron Claw (Columbia, 1941) made his first appearance in silent films, but retained his hideous intrigue in this frantic hidden-door thriller.

Left, Everyone knew that Kenneth MacDonald was behind the mask in *The Valley of Vanishing Men* (Columbia, 1942). George Chesebro watches as MacDonald gives Kenne Duncan a little unfriendly persuasion.

Right, The Black Ace was the deadly leader of the *Mystery Squadron* (Mascot, 1933).

Bottom, With his false hand showing, The Octopus continues to give orders that will bring industrial domination within his grasp in *The Spider's Web* (Columbia, 1938).

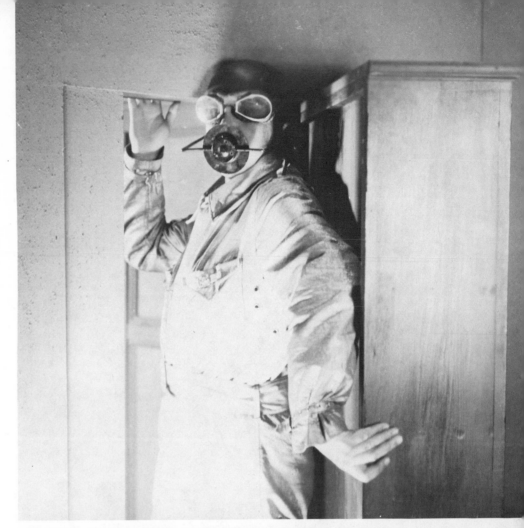

Above, The Crimson Ghost (Republic, 1946) utilized the ruthless services of Clayton Moore and Stanley Price to further his quest for power.

Right, The Skull often seemed to spend more time keeping his men in line than fighting *Deadwood Dick* (Columbia, 1940).

Right, Stanley Price really wasn't a mystery man, but he did have to wear this outfit in *The Invisible Monster* (Republic, 1950) in order to become invisible when a special beam of light was focused on him.

Below, The title character of *The Clutching Hand* (Weiss-Mintz, 1936) gave orders to his men via this television set-up.

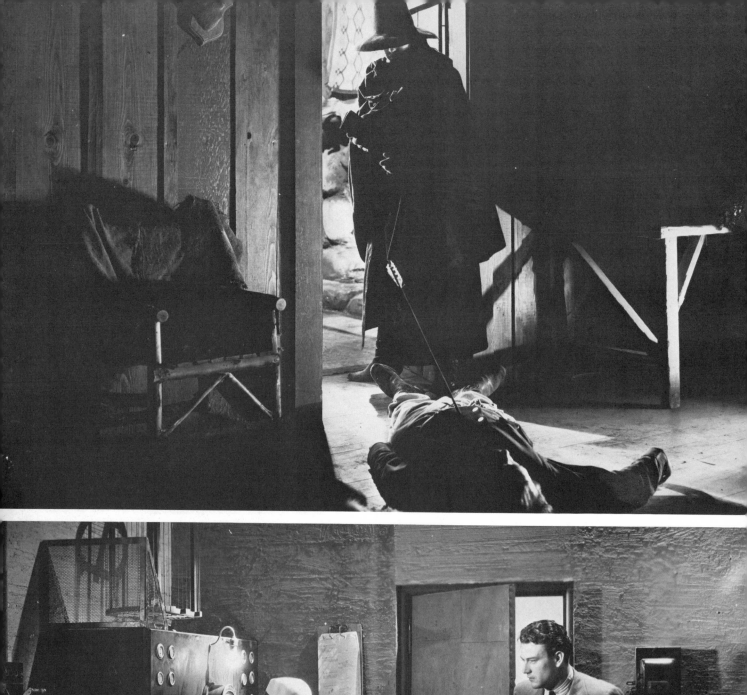

Above, For many serial devotees The Lightning was a favorite masked villain as he unleashed his devastating electrical devices at the *Fighting Devil Dogs* (Republic, 1938).

Top left, The Wolf Man has struck again in the Western thriller *The Lightning Warrior* (Mascot, 1931).

Bottom left, A youthful John Wayne believes he has at last captured The Eagle in *The Shadow of the Eagle* (Mascot, 1932).

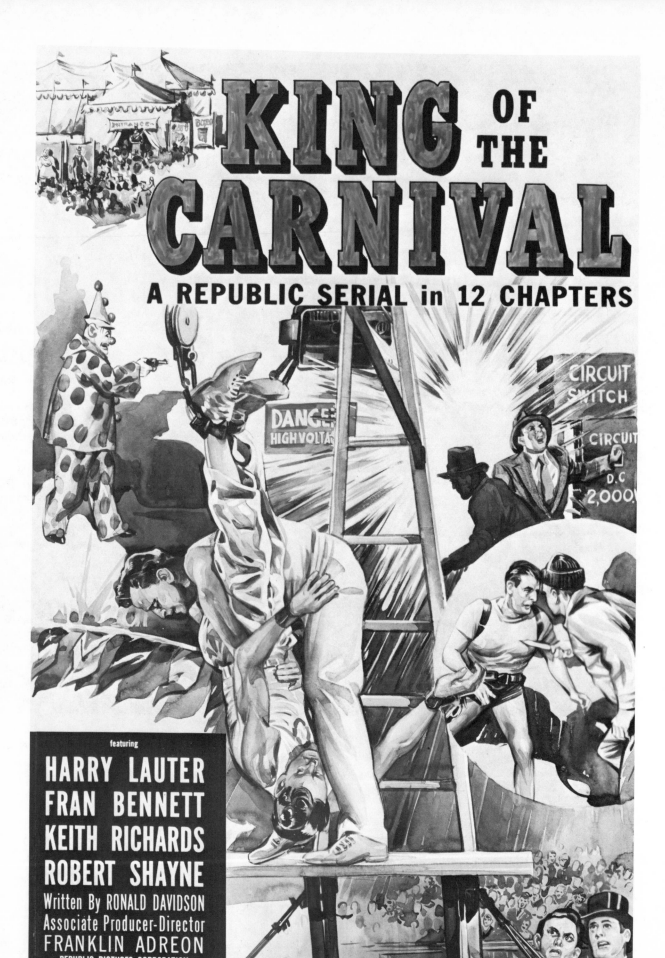

12 THE FINAL FADE-OUT

A CONTINUING RISE in production costs and the emergence of an electronic marvel, television, combined to force the cessation of serial product in 1956 after an uninterrupted run of more than forty years. In the thirties and forties there were thousands of small theaters that could earn a profit by running serials and low-budget films and B-Westerns, but early television offered viewers the same type of material for nothing and within a few short years the once-thriving Saturday matinee market had vanished.

Universal, whose serials in the early forties had always been unimaginative, was the first studio to see the writing on the wall, and wrapped up their serial production in 1946 with *The Mysterious Mr. M*. Universal, wanting to upgrade their image, had decided to concentrate on making better quality features and dropped their B-Western and low-budget feature schedule as well. As far as serial fans were concerned, it really wasn't too great a loss. Titles like *Mystery of the River Boat, The Great Alaskan Mystery* and *Lost City of the Jungle* were over-scripted and boring tales that depended upon stock footage from bigger-budgeted features to provide chapter-ending thrills. No less than three cliffhangers for *Lost City of the Jungle* were based on footage lifted from the Maria Montez and Jon Hall Technicolor adventure, *White Savage*. Things had reached such a sorry state that in Universal's final effort, *The Mysterious Mr. M*, stock material from Republic serials was used to give the film some semblance of quality.

Nine years later when Republic finally called a halt to their production of serials there was evidence of more mixed feelings. The serials had always played an important part in the studio's history. Quality had always been an important concern. Their writers were the best at concocting colorful and exciting screenplays. Their miniature work was the best of any studio, including giants like Warner Bros. and Paramount. They composed original musical scores that were exciting additions to the screen action, with William Lava and Mort Glickman penning the best of the lot. Name any category: directing, set design, camerawork, acting—you will find that Republic was the undisputed champ. They knew what moviegoers and theater owners wanted, and they gave it to them. The studio's quality had reached its zenith in the mid-forties when virtually all their serials had original endings. After that, a greater dependence was placed upon writing endings that would conform to the studio's vast library of special effects. A single new serial would then be basically constructed around two or three earlier efforts. *Trader Tom of the China Seas,* for example, utilized stock endings from *SOS Coast Guard, Haunted Harbor* and *Drums of Fu Manchu.* Although it was a cheap way to give audiences something new, such was the skill of the production staff that these later serials still were fast-paced and exciting (with the possible exception of *Jungle Drums of Africa,* which was an outright bore). The studio that had given us such memorable mystery men as The Scorpion, Don Del Oro and The Lightning decided to give us one last chance to play detective by trying to uncover the mysterious head of a counterfeiting ring in *King of the Carnival.* Harry Lauter, a very capable character actor, became Republic's final leading man as he uncovered the villain, putting an end to his get-rich-quick scheme and capping the studio's twentieth year of cliffhanger production, in 1955.

As Columbia was the last to enter the serial field, so, too, was it the last to leave, also climaxing twenty years of active production, one year later. Columbia's record was a mixed one. They started off poorly with the dreadful *Jungle Menace* in 1937 and then started turning out really first-rate material like *Overland With Kit Carson, The Secret of Treasure Island* and *The Spider's Web.* Then director James Horne took over and serials like *The Iron Claw, Deadwood Dick, The Green Archer* and *The Spider Returns* set serial fans' funny bones in motion with their ludicrous sight gags and ridiculous situations (i.e., gangsters playing jacks, hanging out their laundry, wearing silly party hats, etc.). Columbia certainly seemed to be slipping, but director Spencer Gordon Bennet came to the rescue and turned out twenty of the last twenty-one serials produced by the studio and many of them turned out to be quite entertaining and exciting. Like Republic, these later films were written around stock sequences from earlier features. *Riding With Buffalo Bill* starring Marshall Reed found the hero alternately dressing to match scenes from *Deadwood Dick* and *The Valley of Vanishing Men.* Director Bennet found himself turning out a whole new serial in less than two weeks, when in earlier days it would take two directors almost a full month. Columbia's final production for the matinee crowds was a strictly routine Western adventure starring Lee Roberts and Dennis Moore called *Blazing the Overland Trail.* There would be no new trails to blaze anymore at Columbia, Republic or Universal.

When television first made its impact on the public, the only films available for showing were independent productions and material from smaller companies. Mascot serials and a few titles like *The Clutching Hand, The Black Coin* and *Blake of Scotland Yard,* among others, became regular afternoon viewing fare. The first Republic serials made their debut in edited form in a Captain Midnight television series in which the good Captain would announce that we were going to watch the adventures of one of his agents and would then show *The Crimson Ghost, Son of Zorro* or some similar material. Later, several packages of the complete serials would show up. Universal titles had made an even earlier appearance as afterschool watchers followed the adventures of *Flash Gordon, Buck Rogers,* or *Don Winslow of the Navy* on shows like New York's famous Serial Theater. To my knowledge, the Columbia serials never played on American television, but did show up on Canadian home screens.

In 1965 Columbia released all fifteen chapters of its 1943 *Batman* serial to theaters to screen in a single sitting, after a series of midnight screenings of the title in Chicago had created quite a stir. *Batman,* with its silly stereotypes and preposterous scripting, was well received. Republic, knowing full well that their product was better, tried to cash in on the action by releasing all twelve chapters of their best serial, *Adventures of Captain Marvel,* for similar bookings. The gamble failed. Audiences watched *Batman* because they wanted to laugh at an antique. They didn't laugh at *Adventures of Captain Marvel* because it was too good. Plans to release another of their big hits, *Spy Smasher,* were quietly dropped.

The release of *Batman* did have some positive commercial effect, however. It spawned the popular television series starring Adam West in a heavily burlesqued format in which Batman battled an all-star cast of big-name villains, and it encouraged Republic to edit twenty-six of their serial adventures into 100-minute feature versions, *Fighting Devil Dogs* becoming *The Torpedo of Doom* and *The Black Widow* becoming *Sombra, the Spider Woman,* etc.

1965 also saw a bunch of serial buffs, the author included, get together under the direction of Louis McMahon, a top-flight cameraman, and film a silent satire of the Republic serial format called *Captain Celluloid vs. the Film Pirates.* The result turned out to be so good that prints were eventually made for distribution and wound up playing at many colleges in this country and overseas as well.

As the seventies approached, it appeared that the serial was destined once again to sink into oblivion when a new phenomenon occurred: the nostalgia convention. Meeting yearly in Houston under the guidance of Earl Blair and in Nashville under the auspices of Packy Smith, these gatherings brought in many of the great serial and B-Western stars as guests and featured complete screenings of numerous serial favorites. A new generation was offered the chance to see these classic action favorites, and those who had experienced original magic by first-hand viewing in earlier times were able to have their memories given an emotional booster shot. Stars like Buster Crabbe and Kirk Alyn found themselves in constant demand to travel around the country making guest appearances. And the continued momentum seems, even at this writing, to be building. Public Broadcasting Systems have garnered exceptional audience response by running the *Flash Gordon* serials. In New York when the last chapter of *Zorro's Fighting Legion* was inadvertently cut off the air in early 1976, a storm of protest was encountered and an angry column even appeared in the *New York Daily News.*

There is no chance that serials as we once knew them can ever be duplicated. We have matured too much for that. Like the tinny-sounding phonograph record, the radio adventure show and the Big Little Book, the serial was strictly a product of its time. Now, only the memories of hundreds of Saturday afternoons spent clutching hot bags of popcorn and cheering those bigger-than-life heroes and villains remain. But, ah—what memories!

Right, In *Adventures of Captain Africa* (Columbia, 1955) John Hart was costumed to match earlier footage from *The Phantom* while co-star Rick Vallin donned Gilbert Roland's wardrobe from *The Desert Hawk.*

Below, One of the primary reasons for the demise of the serial was the large number of crew members needed to photograph even simple scenes like this for *Adventures of Captain Africa.* Director Spencer Bennet is seated in the director's chair next to camera.

Left, Marshall Reed, much better known as a B-Western heavy, got a chance to play hero as the star of *Riding with Buffalo Bill* (Columbia, 1954). His costume gives away the fact that stock from the earlier *Deadwood Dick* (Columbia, 1940) will likely be in evidence.

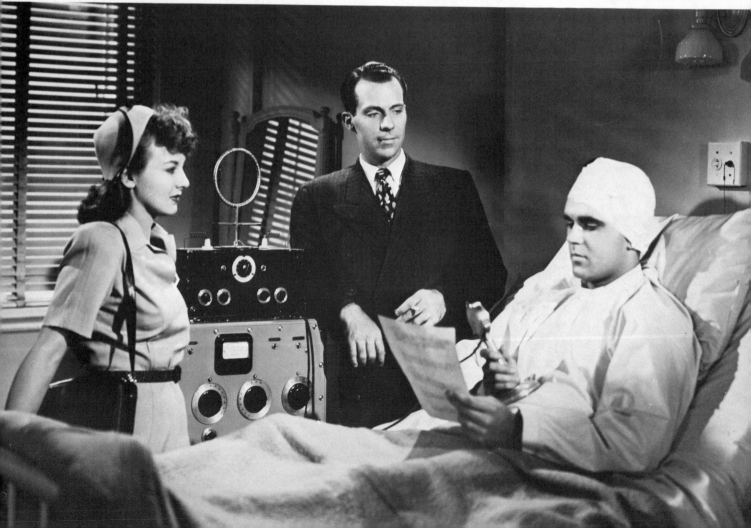

Top left, Dennis Moore, a popular featured player in hundreds of B-Westerns, delivers a telling blow in *Perils of the Wilderness* (Columbia, 1955).

Bottom left, Pamela Blake and Dennis Moore enlist the aid of the injured Richard Martin in Universal's last serial production, *The Mysterious Mr. M* (Universal, 1946).

Right, Bill Kennedy, one of the most ineffectual of all serial heroes, slugs it out with veteran heavy George Eldredge in *The Royal Mounted Rides Again* (Universal, 1945).

Below, Tom Steele, portraying a mute heavy of dubious origin, tries to finish Harry Lauter once and for all in *Trader Tom of the China Seas* (Republic, 1954).

237

Above, A production shot from *Trader Tom of the China Seas* (Republic, 1954) showing how a motor-boat sequence is shot with a process screen behind and a prop man spraying water through a hose up front. Harry Lauter and Aline Towne are in the boat.

Right, Judd Holdren, who had starred in the earlier *Captain Video,* did other-world duty once again in *The Lost Planet* (Columbia, 1953). Assisting Holdren was Ted Thorpe, left.

Left, Bud Osborne, Tommy Farrell and Clay (shortened from Clayton) Moore were the heroes of *Son of Geronimo* (Columbia, 1952).

Below, In *Captain Celluloid vs. The Film Pirates* (Adventure Pictures, 1965) director Louis McMahon successfully copied the style and flavor of the Republic serial in a four-episode silent film which has played all over the world. Alan G. Barbour is doubling under the robe as the Master Duper while his wife, Jean, effectively portrays the evil Satanya.

COMPLETE LIST OF SOUND SERIALS (arranged chronologically by studio)

REPUBLIC PICTURES CORPORATION

TITLE	STAR	NO. OF EPISODES	YEAR
1. *Darkest Africa*	Clyde Beatty	15	1936
2. *Undersea Kingdom*	Ray "Crash" Corrigan	12	
3. *The Vigilantes Are Coming*	Robert Livingston	12	
4. *Robinson Crusoe of Clipper Island*	Mala	14	
5. *Dick Tracy*	Ralph Byrd	15	1937
6. *The Painted Stallion*	Ray "Crash" Corrigan	12	
7. *SOS Coast Guard*	Ralph Byrd	12	
8. *Zorro Rides Again*	John Carroll	12	
9. *The Lone Ranger*	Lee Powell	15	1938
10. *Fighting Devil Dogs*	Lee Powell	12	
11. *Dick Tracy Returns*	Ralph Byrd	15	
12. *Hawk of the Wilderness*	Herman Brix	12	
13. *The Lone Ranger Rides Again*	Robert Livingston	15	1939
14. *Daredevils of the Red Circle*	Charles Quigley	12	
15. *Dick Tracy's G-Men*	Ralph Byrd	15	
16. *Zorro's Fighting Legion*	Reed Hadley	12	
17. *Drums of Fu Manchu*	Henry Brandon	15	1940
18. *Adventures of Red Ryder*	Don "Red" Barry	12	
19. *King of the Royal Mounted*	Allan Lane	12	
20. *Mysterious Doctor Satan*	Eduardo Ciannelli	15	
21. *Adventures of Captain Marvel*	Tom Tyler	12	1941
22. *Jungle Girl*	Frances Gifford	15	
23. *King of the Texas Rangers*	"Slingin' Sammy" Baugh	12	
24. *Dick Tracy vs. Crime, Inc.*	Ralph Byrd	15	
25. *Spy Smasher*	Kane Richmond	12	1942
26. *Perils of Nyoka*	Kay Aldridge	15	
27. *King of the Mounties*	Allan Lane	12	
28. *G-Men vs. The Black Dragon*	Rod Cameron	15	1943
29. *Daredevils of the West*	Allan Lane	12	
30. *Secret Service in Darkest Africa*	Rod Cameron	15	
31. *The Masked Marvel*	William Forrest	12	
32. *Captain America*	Dick Purcell	15	1944
33. *The Vigilante*	Ralph Byrd	15	
34. *Haunted Harbor*	Kane Richmond	15	
35. *Zorro's Black Whip*	George J. Lewis	12	
36. *Manhunt of Mystery Island*	Richard Bailey	15	1945
37. *Federal Operator 99*	Marten Lamont	12	
38. *The Purple Monster Strikes*	Dennis Moore	15	
39. *The Phantom Rider*	Robert Kent	12	1946
40. *King of the Forest Rangers*	Larry Thompson	12	
41. *Daughter of Don Q*	Adrian Booth	12	
42. *The Crimson Ghost*	Charles Quigley	12	
43. *Son of Zorro*	George Turner	13	1947
44. *Jesse James Rides Again*	Clayton Moore	13	
45. *The Black Widow*	Bruce Edwards	13	
46. *G-Men Never Forget*	Clayton Moore	12	1948

TITLE	STAR	NO. OF EPISODES	YEAR
47. *Dangers of the Canadian Mounted*	Jim Bannon	12	
48. *Adventures of Frank and Jesse James*	Clayton Moore	13	
49. *Federal Agents vs. Underworld, Inc.*	Kirk Alyn	12	1949
50. *Ghost of Zorro*	Clayton Moore	12	
51. *King of the Rocket Men*	Tristram Coffin	12	
52. *The James Brothers of Missouri*	Keith Richards	12	1950
53. *Radar Patrol vs. Spy King*	Kirk Alyn	12	
54. *The Invisible Monster*	Richard Webb	12	
55. *Desperadoes of the West*	Richard Powers	12	
56. *Flying Disc Man from Mars*	Walter Reed	12	1951
57. *Don Daredevil Rides Again*	Ken Curtis	12	
58. *Government Agents vs. Phantom Legion*	Walter Reed	12	
59. *Radar Men from the Moon*	George Wallace	12	1952
60. *Zombies of the Stratosphere*	Judd Holdren	12	
61. *Jungle Drums of Africa*	Clay Moore	12	1953
62. *Canadian Mounties vs. Atomic Invaders*	Bill Henry	12	
63. *Trader Tom of the China Seas*	Harry Lauter	12	1954
64. *Man with the Steel Whip*	Richard Simmons	12	
65. *Panther Girl of the Kongo*	Phyllis Coates	12	1955
66. *King of the Carnival*	Harry Lauter	12	

COLUMBIA PICTURES CORPORATION

TITLE	STAR	NO. OF EPISODES	YEAR
1. *Jungle Menace*	Frank Buck	15	1937
2. *The Mysterious Pilot*	Captain Frank Hawks	15	
3. *The Secret of Treasure Island*	Don Terry	15	1938
4. *The Great Adventures of Wild Bill Hickok*	Gordon Elliott	15	
5. *The Spider's Web*	Warren Hull	15	
6. *Flying G-Men*	Robert Paige	15	1939
7. *Mandrake, the Magician*	Warren Hull	12	
8. *Overland with Kit Carson*	Bill Elliott	15	
9. *The Shadow*	Victor Jory	15	1940
10. *Terry and the Pirates*	William Tracy	15	
11. *Deadwood Dick*	Don Douglas	15	
12. *The Green Archer*	Victor Jory	15	
13. *White Eagle*	Buck Jones	15	1941
14. *The Spider Returns*	Warren Hull	15	
15. *The Iron Claw*	Charles Quigley	15	
16. *Holt of the Secret Service*	Jack Holt	15	
17. *Captain Midnight*	Dave O'Brien	15	1942
18. *Perils of the Royal Mounted*	Robert Stevens	15	
19. *The Secret Code*	Paul Kelly	15	
20. *The Valley of Vanishing Men*	Bill Elliott	15	
21. *Batman*	Lewis Wilson	15	1943
22. *The Phantom*	Tom Tyler	15	
23. *The Desert Hawk*	Gilbert Roland	15	1944
24. *Black Arrow*	Robert Scott	15	
25. *Brenda Starr, Reporter*	Joan Woodbury	13	1945
26. *The Monster and the Ape*	Robert Lowery	15	
27. *Jungle Raiders*	Kane Richmond	15	
28. *Who's Guilty?*	Robert Kent	15	
29. *Hop Harrigan*	William Bakewell	15	1946
30. *Chick Carter, Detective*	Lyle Talbot	15	

TITLE	STAR	NO. OF EPISODES	YEAR
31. *Son of the Guardsman*	Robert Shaw	15	
32. *Jack Armstrong*	John Hart	15	*1947*
33. *The Vigilante*	Ralph Byrd	15	
34. *The Sea Hound*	Buster Crabbe	15	
35. *Brick Bradford*	Kane Richmond	15	
36. *Tex Granger*	Robert Kellard	15	*1948*
37. *Superman*	Kirk Alyn	15	
38. *Congo Bill*	Don McGuire	15	
39. *Bruce Gentry*	Tom Neal	15	*1949*
40. *Batman and Robin*	Robert Lowery	15	
41. *Adventures of Sir Galahad*	George Reeves	15	
42. *Cody of the Pony Express*	Jock O'Mahoney	15	*1950*
43. *Atom Man vs. Superman*	Kirk Alyn	15	
44. *Pirates of the High Seas*	Buster Crabbe	15	
45. *Roar of the Iron Horse*	Jock O'Mahoney	15	*1951*
46. *Mysterious Island*	Richard Crane	15	
47. *Captain Video*	Judd Holdren	15	
48. *King of the Congo*	Buster Crabbe	15	*1952*
49. *Blackhawk*	Kirk Alyn	15	
50. *Son of Geronimo*	Clay Moore	15	
51. *The Lost Planet*	Judd Holdren	15	*1953*
52. *The Great Adventures of Captain Kidd*	Richard Crane	15	
53. *Gunfighters of the Northwest*	Jack Mahoney	15	*1954*
54. *Riding with Buffalo Bill*	Marshall Reed	15	
55. *Adventures of Captain Africa*	John Hart	15	*1955*
56. *Perils of the Wilderness*	Dennis Moore	15	*1956*
57. *Blazing the Overland Trail*	Lee Roberts	15	

UNIVERSAL PICTURES

TITLE	STAR	NO. OF EPISODES	YEAR
1. *Ace of Scotland Yard* silent & part-talkie versions	Crauford Kent	10	*1929*
2. *Tarzan, the Tiger* silent & sound versions	Frank Merrill	15	
3. *The Jade Box* silent & sound versions	Jack Perrin	10	*1930*
4. *The Lightning Express* silent & sound versions	Louise Lorraine	10	
5. *Terry of the Times* silent & sound versions	Reed Howes	10	
6. *The Indians Are Coming* all-talkie and silent versions	Tim McCoy	12	
7. *Finger Prints*	Kenneth Harlan	10	*1931*
8. *Heroes of the Flames*	Tim McCoy	12	
9. *Danger Island*	Kenneth Harlan	12	
10. *Battling with Buffalo Bill*	Tom Tyler	12	
11. *Spell of the Circus*	Francis X. Bushman, Jr.	10	
12. *Detective Lloyd*	Jack Lloyd	12	*1932*
13. *The Airmail Mystery*	James Flavin	12	
14. *Heroes of the West*	Noah Beery, Jr.	12	
15. *The Jungle Mystery*	Tom Tyler	12	
16. *The Lost Special*	Frank Albertson	12	
17. *Clancy of the Mounted*	Tom Tyler	12	*1933*

TITLE	STAR	NO. OF EPISODES	YEAR
18. *The Phantom of the Air*	Tom Tyler	12	
19. *Gordon of Ghost City*	Buck Jones	12	
20. *Perils of Pauline*	Evalyn Knapp	12	1934
21. *Pirate Treasure*	Richard Talmadge	12	
22. *The Vanishing Shadow*	Onslow Stevens	12	
23. *The Red Rider*	Buck Jones	15	
24. *Tailspin Tommy*	Maurice Murphy	12	
25. *Rustlers of Red Dog*	John Mack Brown	12	1935
26. *The Call of the Savage*	Noah Beery, Jr.	12	
27. *The Roaring West*	Buck Jones	15	
28. *Tailspin Tommy in the Great Air Mystery*	Clark Williams	12	
29. *The Adventures of Frank Merriwell*	Don Briggs	12	1936
30. *Flash Gordon*	Buster Crabbe	13	
31. *The Phantom Rider*	Buck Jones	15	
32. *Ace Drummond*	John King	13	
33. *Jungle Jim*	Grant Withers	12	1937
34. *Secret Agent X-9*	Scott Kolk	12	
35. *Wild West Days*	John Mack Brown	13	
36. *Radio Patrol*	Grant Withers	12	
37. *Tim Tyler's Luck*	Frankie Thomas	12	
38. *Flash Gordon's Trip to Mars*	Buster Crabbe	15	1938
39. *Flaming Frontiers*	John Mack Brown	15	
40. *Red Barry*	Buster Crabbe	13	
41. *Scouts to the Rescue*	Jackie Cooper	12	1939
42. *Buck Rogers*	Buster Crabbe	12	
43. *The Oregon Trail*	John Mack Brown	15	
44. *The Phantom Creeps*	Bela Lugosi	12	
45. *The Green Hornet*	Gordon Jones	13	1940
46. *Flash Gordon Conquers the Universe*	Buster Crabbe	12	
47. *Winners of the West*	Dick Foran	13	
48. *Junior G-Men*	The Dead End Kids	12	
49. *The Green Hornet Strikes Again*	Warren Hull	15	
50. *Sky Raiders*	Donald Woods	12	1941
51. *Riders of Death Valley*	Dick Foran	15	
52. *Sea Raiders*	The Dead End Kids	12	
53. *Don Winslow of the Navy*	Don Terry	12	1942
54. *Gang Busters*	Kent Taylor	13	
55. *Junior G-Men of the Air*	The Dead End Kids	12	
56. *Overland Mail*	Lon Chaney, Jr.	15	
57. *Adventures of Smilin' Jack*	Tom Brown	13	1943
58. *Don Winslow of the Coast Guard*	Don Terry	13	
59. *Adventures of the Flying Cadets*	Johnny Downs	13	
60. *The Great Alaskan Mystery*	Ralph Morgan	13	1944
61. *Raiders of Ghost City*	Dennis Moore	13	
62. *Mystery of the River Boat*	Robert Lowery	13	
63. *Jungle Queen*	Lois Collier	13	1945
64. *The Master Key*	Milburn Stone	13	
65. *Secret Agent X-9*	Lloyd Bridges	13	
66. *The Royal Mounted Rides Again*	Bill Kennedy	13	
67. *The Scarlet Horseman*	Peter Cookson	13	1946
68. *Lost City of the Jungle*	Russell Hayden	13	
69. *The Mysterious Mr. M*	Richard Martin	13	

TITLE	STAR	NO. OF EPISODES	YEAR

MASCOT PICTURES

1. *King of the Kongo* silent & part-talkie versions	Walter Miller	10	*1929*
2. *The Lone Defender*	Rin-Tin-Tin	12	*1930*
3. *The Phantom of the West*	Tom Tyler	10	
4. *King of the Wild*	Walter Miller	12	
5. *The Vanishing Legion*	Harry Carey	12	*1931*
6. *The Galloping Ghost*	Harold "Red" Grange	12	
7. *The Lightning Warrior*	Rin-Tin-Tin	12	
8. *The Shadow of the Eagle*	John Wayne	12	*1932*
9. *Last of the Mohicans*	Harry Carey	12	
10. *The Hurricane Express*	John Wayne	12	
11. *The Devil Horse*	Harry Carey	12	
12. *The Whispering Shadow*	Bela Lugosi	12	*1933*
13. *The Three Musketeers*	John Wayne	12	
14. *Fighting with Kit Carson*	John Mack Brown	12	
15. *The Wolf Dog*	Rin-Tin-Tin, Jr.	12	
16. *Mystery Squadron*	Bob Steele	12	
17. *The Lost Jungle*	Clyde Beatty	12	*1934*
18. *Burn 'Em Up Barnes*	Jack Mulhall	12	
19. *The Law of the Wild*	Rin-Tin-Tin, Jr.	12	
20. *Mystery Mountain*	Ken Maynard	12	
21. *Phantom Empire*	Gene Autry	12	*1935*
22. *The Miracle Rider*	Tom Mix	15	
23. *The Adventures of Rex and Rinty*	Rin-Tin-Tin, Jr.	12	
24. *Fighting Marines*	Grant Withers	12	

INDEPENDENT SERIALS

1. *Voice from the Sky (Ben Wilson release)*	Wally Wales	10	*1930*
2. *Mystery Trooper (Syndicate Pictures Corp. release)*	Robert Frazer	10	*1931*
3. *Sign of the Wolf (Metropolitan release)*	Rex Lease	10	
4. *The Last Frontier (RKO-Radio release)*	Lon Chaney, Jr.	12	*1932*
5. *Tarzan, the Fearless (Principal release)*	Buster Crabbe	12	*1933*
6. *The Return of Chandu (Principal release)*	Bela Lugosi	12	*1934*
7. *Young Eagles (First Division)*	Jim Vance	12	
8. *Queen of the Jungle (Screen Attractions Corp. release)*	Reed Howes	12	*1935*
9. *The Lost City (Krellberg release)*	Kane Richmond	12	
10. *The New Adventures of Tarzan (Burroughs-Tarzan release)*	Herman Brix	12	
11. *Custer's Last Stand (Stage and Screen release)*	Rex Lease	15	*1936*
12. *The Clutching Hand (Stage and Screen release)*	Jack Mulhall	15	
13. *The Black Coin (Stage and Screen release)*	Ralph Graves	15	
14. *Shadow of Chinatown (Victory release)*	Bela Lugosi	15	
15. *Blake of Scotland Yard (Victory release)*	Ralph Byrd	15	*1937*